ASSESSING LEARNING
Standards, Principles, and Procedures

Second Edition

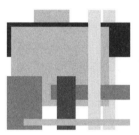

Morry Fiddler
Catherine Marienau
Urban Whitaker

with a foreword by David O. Justice

CAEL

The Council for Adult & Experiential Learning
Chicago

KENDALL/HUNT PUBLISHING COMPANY
4050 Westmark Drive   Dubuque, Iowa 52002

CAEL

The Council for Adult & Experiential Learning
55 East Monroe Street, Suite 1930
Chicago, Illinois 60603

For Morris Keeton
With deepest respect and appreciation

Contents

Foreword

During the seventeen years since the publication of Urban Whitaker's book, *Assessing Learning: Standards, Principles, and Practices,* the landscape of higher education (and adult learning) has changed dramatically. The "nontraditional" adult student has become traditional. Companies have launched training divisions (often labeled "universities") with chief learning officers and extensive programs for all levels of employees. For-profit providers have joined the ranks of main line higher education, bringing a new level of sophistication to marketing and a special focus on adult learner services. Online learning has become the fastest growing channel through which working adults can learn while maintaining a full-time work schedule. Increasingly in the corporate environment learning is being recognized as a necessary component for growth, efficiency, and innovation. And in higher education it is now widely acknowledged that learning cannot stop with the award of an associate's or a bachelor's degree. Indeed, lifelong learning is now commonly recognized as a foundation for a democratic and open society. As lifelong learning becomes more commonplace and accessible, the centrality of assessing learning will also grow because we have learned that individuals do not necessarily learn the same thing from the same experience. At the same time it is no longer accepted that a diploma or a certificate, without some convincing backup, qualifies an individual for a promotion or a serious responsibility. Real knowledge is the key to both personal and professional success. And valid and reliable assessment is the foundational component for programs that can promote such success.

Seventeen years ago in his foreword to the first edition of Whitaker's book, Morris Keeton noted, "A particularly troublesome aspect of the surge of enrollments by adults 25 years and older has been the increase of incompetent or unethical purveyors of 'credit for life experience programs and services.'" While abuses in the awarding of academic credit still persist, this book has made a major contribution to curtailing such programs by providing a set of standards for the assessment of learning and the awarding of credit for learning gained from experience. Adopted in whole or in part by several regional accrediting bodies, the CAEL "Ten Standards for Quality Assurance" are internationally recognized as the best way to ensure that reliability and quality is maintained while real learning is appropriately recognized. In England, Canada, South Africa, and Australia, to mention only the most explicitly and actively connected, recognition of learning from experience has become integral to the reforms of educational systems on which they have embarked. And the CAEL standards for the assessment of learning have significantly contributed to the formation of these national policies.

The re-issuance of this hallmark CAEL publication signals a continuing commitment to the CAEL tradition of promoting experiential learning pioneered by Morris Keeton more than 30 years ago. Since then Morris has substantively contributed to many CAEL publications, and he has been an inspiration for the others. This book too has benefited from Morris's ideas, experience, and vision. As he so clearly and unambiguously stated in the foreword for the original edition of *Assessing Learning,* ". . . I hope that academics and trainers everywhere will take seriously the need for valid and reliable assessment of the learning outcomes of their work. A teacher or trainer who does not know what students are gaining from the instruction or training provided is also unable to plan intelligently to improve instruction." It is this dual role of ensuring the quality of the programs relying on the standards articulated in the book and stimulating further learning on the part of the instructor or trainer and the learner that makes this book especially valuable. And it is the tradition of Morris's commitment to innovation and quality.

By retaining the name and the original author's place we intend to both recognize the groundbreaking contribution Urban Whitaker made to assessing learning and to signal the continuity of purpose and goal that has been CAEL from its inception in 1974. While there are significant changes in the text, the original formatting is retained and most of the standards remain intact.

It is in the same spirit of commitment to lifelong learning and the accurate and fair assessment of learning gained from whatever source, that CAEL commissioned this revised version of *Assessing Learning.* In this version, Morry Fiddler and Catherine Marienau, professors in DePaul University's School for New Learning, have incorporated many of the "best practices" gained from their research in adult learning theory and practice as well as their own experiences in assessing learning for adults in both graduate and undergraduate programs. Indeed Catherine and Morry are also the creators of the first online Prior Learning Assessment Certificate program offered by CAEL beginning in fall of 1998. While respecting the Whitaker framework and the fundamental principles, they have added important perspectives and contexts that bring assessment of learning to new venues, including work-based learning and non-credit-based learning.

In addition to explicating and elaborating (and in two instances modifying) the ten standards in light of the many changes of the past fifteen years, the authors also tie in many of the new and emerging environments for lifelong learning and make more explicit the connection between effective assessment and learning itself. They place special emphasis on the connection between self-assessment and conscious and explicit engagement of the learner in developing new learning goals and the plans to attain them. This is an important connection and one that deserves more attention than many administrators tend to give it. If the larger goal is to enhance learning, then understanding how assessment can contribute to learning is an equally important goal.

Finally it is important to view this new version of *Assessing Learning* from the perspective of the growing demand to control the costs of higher education at a time when consumers are expecting prices to hold constant or drop rather than constantly increase at a rate above the consumer index. By integrating the knowledge, skills, and learning adults have gained through a wide range of work and life experiences, institutions can reduce the amount of time and effort (hence costs) put into the awarding of a degree for many individuals. And, if done in conformity to the standards set forth in this book, they can do it without compromising the quality of the outcomes.

This book should be of value to a wide range of individuals. It will help faculty who may be asked to assess the knowledge of an adult learner. It can assist administrators called upon to ensure consistency in compliance with institutional rules and regulations. And it can open new opportunities for corporate information and training officers seeking to maximize the use of available knowledge within their company. By focusing on learning and the attainment of identified learning outcomes, this version of *Assessing Learning* will be even more useful for trainers in nonacademic settings without reducing its applicability to institutions of higher education.

David O. Justice
Vice President for Lifelong Learning
DePaul University
January 10, 2006

Ten Standards for Assessing Learning

I. Credit or its equivalent should be awarded only for *learning,* and not for *experience.*

II. Assessment should be based on standards and criteria for the level of acceptable learning that are both agreed upon and made public.

III. Assessment should be treated as an integral part of learning, not separate from it, and should be based on an understanding of learning processes.

IV. The determination of credit awards and competence levels must be made by appropriate subject matter and academic or credentialing experts.

V. Credit or other credentialing should be appropriate to the context in which it is awarded and accepted.

VI. If awards are for credit, transcript entries should clearly describe what learning is being recognized and should be monitored to avoid giving credit twice for the same learning.

VII. Policies, procedures, and criteria applied to assessment, including provision for appeal, should be fully disclosed and prominently available to all parties involved in the assessment process.

VIII. Fees charged for assessment should be based on the services performed in the process and not determined by the amount of credit awarded.

IX. All personnel involved in the assessment of learning should pursue and receive adequate training and continuing professional development for the functions they perform.

X. Assessment programs should be regularly monitored, reviewed, evaluated, and revised as needed to reflect changes in the needs being served, the purposes being met, and the state of the assessment arts.

CHAPTER

1

Definitions, Propositions, and Assumptions

All of us are lifelong experiential learners. That we are is compelling, if not always acknowledged. Empirical research has shown that experiential learning methods often produce superior learning outcomes compared with direct instruction and that the conversion of experience into knowledge is a complex, multifaceted, and unique process. So the issue is not whether there will be experiential learning, but rather, how effective it will be and how such learning should be assessed.

> Experiential learning is not a matter of if, but how well

These basic issues give rise to three priorities for facilitators of learning (e.g., educators, trainers, mentors, managers, leaders) and learners alike: *(a)* "learning how to learn from experience" emerges as a major objective for education—at all levels; *(b)* achieving a blend of learning activities and strategies that fit the learning needs and each individual's learning style becomes a daily requirement; and *(c)* integrating assessment into the learning and evaluation processes requires intentional effort. These three educational propositions serve as appropriate starting points for considering the assessment of learning.

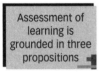

> Assessment of learning is grounded in three propositions

Learning how to learn from experience is not an easy task. It is made more difficult by the fact that doing so is only rarely recognized as a primary educational objective. It is highlighted here because the process of assessment itself provides a primary opportunity for learning how to learn. Through the feedback process that good assessment provides in various forms, learning can be affirmed, amended, and extended. While this is true for any form of learning, it is particularly the case for learning that is derived from experience. It offers both process and content information to assist new learning. From the process perspective, awareness of the strengths and weaknesses of the learner's approaches can lead to intentional improvements in the regulation of learning. From the content perspective, identifying the quality of learning provides

> Affirming, amending, and extending . . . three qualities of feedback

an essential foundation for setting new objectives that can expand the quantity of learning as well.

The blending of experiential and externally structured (e.g., classroom) learning is not a new phenomenon. It has been done, and done well, in the workplace and in formal educational contexts through cooperative education, internships, and other field and laboratory programs for a long time. But if the assessment practices in these programs are inadequately developed, much can be lost or missed. And the rapid growth in experiential learning activities of all kinds has created an urgent need for statements of assessment standards, principles, and procedures.

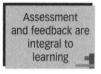
Assessment and feedback are integral to learning

Nearly all theories of learning predict that some sort of reinforcing or corrective feedback will enhance learning in whatever manner it occurs. This supports a fundamental premise that assessment should be integrated into any learning process. Recognizing that learning occurs in multiple dimensions (e.g., perceptual, cognitive, affective, and behavioral), attention to sound assessment processes and practices becomes both a requisite and a reward for anyone seriously interested in promoting learning—one's own as well as that of others.

Forms of Learning

Though the emphasis of this book is on the assessment of learning gained through experience, we have retained the title *Assessing Learning* for this edition rather than *Assessing Experiential Learning.* We did so because the rules for assessment are essentially the same for all types of

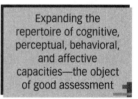
Expanding the repertoire of cognitive, perceptual, behavioral, and affective capacities—the object of good assessment

learning. To learn is to acquire knowledge or skill. To assess is to identify the level of knowledge or skill that has been acquired (i.e., the outcomes). Acquiring learning and assessing learning are interdependent processes. It is particularly important to realize that assessment, undertaken creatively and with rigor, promotes additional learning and expands the repertoire of cognitive, perceptual, behavioral, and affective capacities.[1]

There are, of course, multiple ways to describe learning depending on the context of the conversation; the "language" of learning is more or less

---

[1] These four dimensions are grounded in David Kolb's theory of experiential learning and development and in his model of effective learning. The model—best known as the *learning cycle*—features four modes of learning: experience, reflection, abstraction, and experimentation. In order for learning to be most effective, these four modes need to be engaged in some way during the learning process. His theory, in brief, posits that learning (the kind that stimulates development) is a dialectical process that involves recognizing and dealing with life's

differentiated, more or less precise, depending on the milieu (e.g., research, personal development, the workplace, therapy, or education). Because the assessment of learning depends on the measurement of learning outcomes, we separate types of learning into two categories based on these different outcomes—they are *reproductive learning* and *reconstructive learning*.

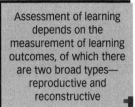

Assessment of learning depends on the measurement of learning outcomes, of which there are two broad types—reproductive and reconstructive

Reproductive learning is marked by memorization and reproduction of information. Reconstructive learning is marked by understanding, application, viewing information in context(s) from different perspectives, and change as a person[2] (i.e., meaningful learning that can be characterized further as beliefs, significance, action, or connections to other knowledge).

Each of these forms of learning leads to differing strategies and techniques for assessment. It is rare that learning outcomes may be characterized as solely reproductive or reconstructive. It is not so rare, however, that assessment practices reinforce and even reward one or the other unintentionally. The aim may be learning that is reconstructive, but the assessment practices may reinforce and reward reproductive learning, and thus miss measuring what matters most.

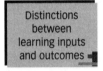

Distinctions between learning inputs and outcomes

These differing forms of learning can be subdivided in a variety of ways while still reinforcing the importance of distinguishing between the learning *inputs* and the *outcomes*. A brief look at the distinction between common classroom learning and experiential learning illustrates this. James Coleman has analyzed the differences in the following way:[3]

Information assimilation (classroom learning):

1. Receiving information (through symbolic sources such as lectures or reading)

---

contradictions and resolving them through various types of adaptations. These adaptations involve cognitive, perceptual, behavioral, and affective capacities, which an individual might engage at different levels of maturity depending on the complexity, context, and novelty of the situation. For a practitioner's interpretation of Kolb's theory/model, see Taylor, Fiddler, & Marienau, *Developing Adult Learners* (San Francisco: Jossey-Bass, 2000, 22–30; 337–340). In order to fully appreciate Kolb's contributions to theory and practice regarding experiential learning and development, see the original source: *Experiential Learning* (Englewood Cliffs, NJ: Prentice Hall, 1984).

[2] Ference Marton and Shirley Booth, *Learning and Awareness* (Mahwah, NJ: Erlbaum, 1997), 37–38.

[3] Cited in Morris T. Keeton & Associates, *Experiential Learning: Rationale, Characteristics, and Assessment* (San Francisco: Jossey-Bass, 1976), 49–61.

2. Assimilating and organizing information so that a general principle is understood
3. Applying the general principle in specific instances
4. Applying the general principle in new circumstances

Experiential learning:

1. Acting and observing
2. Understanding the effects of the action in a specific instance
3. Understanding the general principle
4. Applying the general principle in new circumstances

The most important difference cited by Coleman is the source of information. In common classroom learning, the source is "symbolic"—such as listening to lectures or reading (though both are also experiences). In experiential learning, the source of information is "acting" or "observing": that is, something the learner does, or watches somebody else do, rather than something the learner hears or reads about.

According to Coleman, the difference in the *source* of information leads to a vital difference in the learning *process*—it is more deductive when information comes from traditional sources such as lectures or libraries, and more inductive when information comes from acting or observing action.

These distinctions are useful, but their utility is in describing the process of acquiring learning, not in the process of assessing it. The essential difference is in the education input, rather than in the learning outcomes.

Experiential Learning, Learning from Experience

Though the two phrases "experiential learning" and "learning from experience" are often used interchangeably, they are not identical. Here, the distinction between inputs and outcomes again comes in handy. Experiential learning is more often associated with the nature of learning activities[4] themselves, while learning from experience is the outcome of processes (i.e., what meaning something holds) that live in tandem with experiential learning. Upon reviewing a

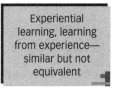

Experiential learning, learning from experience— similar but not equivalent

---

[4] Morris T. Keeton and Pamela Tate have defined experiential learning as learning in which the learner is directly in touch with the realities being studied. Morris T. Keeton and Pamela Tate, *New Directions for Experiential Learning: Learning by Experience What, Why, How* (San Francisco: Jossey-Bass, 1978), 2.

wide body of literature, Sheckley and Keeton[5] derived six principles of adult learning, two of which directly address these considerations:

- A rich body of experience is essential for learning to occur best.
- Experience yields explicit knowledge only if reflected upon.

Probably the most challenging aspects of assessing learning are related to learning gained through nonacademic events—structured events that are experiential—and learning from life's experiences generally, especially when they need to be translated into academic credit. These nonacademic events are often manifestations of reconstructive learning because of the individualized meanings the outcomes may hold. In the academic context, these events are more likely to be seen among adults returning to school or in situations that require demonstration of knowledge and skills for certification purposes. Before moving on to assessment per se, this supposition makes it worthwhile to give some consideration to both the nature of learning from experience and adults' learning generally. Such attention serves as an entrée to principles and procedures for assessing learning in the classroom as well as learning gained from experience.

The elements and processes that combine to drive reconstructive learning derived from experience are illustrated below (figure 1.1).[6]

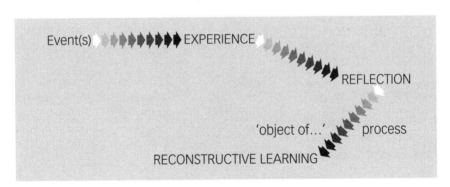

FIGURE 1.1 ▣ A MODEL OF LEARNING FROM EXPERIENCE

---

[5] Barry Sheckley and Morris T. Keeton, *Perspectives on Key Principles of Adult Learning*. (Chicago: CAEL, 1999).

[6] Adapted from Catherine Marienau and Morry Fiddler (2002, December) "Reflection across the Curriculum—by Promoting Learning from Experience." *About Campus* (December 2002): 13–19.

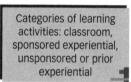

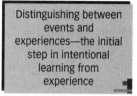

The assessment of experientially gained knowledge, as well as the learning itself, is mediated by reflection (experience yields explicit knowledge only if reflected upon). Reflection may be described as having two components: the object of reflection (the aspects of experiences to which a person pays attention) and the process of reflection (how someone will be thinking about the object of reflection).

This model also distinguishes between an event in one's life and one's experience of it—between being an actor or observer in some occurrence and an interpreter of it. These two dimensions are frequently conflated; in doing so, there is a significant risk that the learner or assessor might depersonalize the meaning-making process and miss the assessment of what actually has been learned. Recognizing the experience(s) in life's events requires attention to the details and the senses (e.g., asking oneself, "What, in fact, did I notice?"). Recognizing the experience in an event is itself a reflective act and most certainly varies from person to person, even among those present at the same event.

Types of Learning Activities

Classroom learning, often referred to as *traditional learning*, is typically a teacher-directed activity. As such, it prescribes a set of norms for expected learning outcomes.

Sponsored experiential learning—such as cooperative education, hands-on training, service learning, and internships—is usually a mix of teacher-directed/supervised and self-directed events.

Finally, *unsponsored experiential*, including prior experiential learning, is distinguished from the other types of learning activities by the absence of external direction. It is often unplanned and cumulative, and its structure is markedly different from a predesigned and delivered curriculum. An important exception to this, however, may be when work experience is involved; in this instance, it is possible, even likely, that aspects of the learning have been facilitated by others (e.g., job supervisors or trainers).

While some aspects of generalized rules for assessment may vary depending upon the learning activity, the primary implication of differentiating types of learning for assessment purposes is simple—it is the outcomes of learning that are the raison d'etre for assessment, not the inputs. The failure to distinguish between the sources and the outcomes of learning is probably the most common misstep in assessment activities.

The Assessment Process

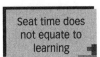

The relationship between the type of learning activity and its assessment presents two temptations that often lead to serious errors in assessment. First, and most seriously, there is the temptation to confuse educational inputs with learning outcomes. The most common instance of this error in classroom learning is the inclusion of "seat time" (attendance) in the determination of a grade (and, hence, of credit). In sponsored experiential learning, for example, this error surfaces when internships are evaluated in terms of the number of "hours per week." The same error often occurs in portfolio evaluation of largely undirected or self-directed prior learning when evaluators equate years of experience with units of credit.

Seat time does not equate to learning

In all three cases, the error is the assumption that time spent leads to learning acquired. When credit is granted for input rather than for outcomes, the assessment process is short-circuited and credit is given for experience rather than for learning.

Teacher-directed learning may or may not be congruent with either an institution's or an individual's objectives

A second problem, particularly with teacher-directed learning, arises from the temptation to overvalue the directing facilitator's personal conception of the learning objectives. For example, in a course on twentieth century history one instructor may emphasize social history, another political history, and another economic history. While the institutional (and perhaps the learner's) objective may be a balanced and general knowledge, the individual instructor's concept may be quite different. The assessment is accordingly affected. This second problem area is, of course, related to the first. Assessment is distorted by the learning director's inputs: determining the content of lectures, choosing library assignments, approving particular internships or sites for work and learning, or evaluating the experiences described in a prior learning portfolio.

Learning activities are easily confused with desired learning outcomes

Effective assessment is enhanced by clarity of learning objectives. In teacher-directed learning, there is maximum opportunity for clear statement of objectives in advance of both the learning and its assessment. Unfortunately, this opportunity is not always realized, as a glance at almost any college catalog will show: "A Survey of American History, 1900–1950" is more descriptive of a possible learning *activity* than it is of any particular learning objective or outcome.

Rules for Assessing Learning

The first requirement for ensuring the quality of learning assessment is to identify some rules for describing acceptable outcomes. The second requirement is to create some basic practices that will lead to the sound measurement and evaluation of those outcomes. And, finally, some guidance should be provided for developing local procedures to implement effective practices.

This sets up a three-tiered approach that is described in the title of this work as "standards, principles, and procedures." The overarching aims are to achieve quality assurance and maintain rigorous academic standards without losing the advantages of flexibility for experimentation and growth. And we sought to have the advantages of both rigor and flexibility by respecting the dividing line between ends (standards of quality) and means (general principles and flexible procedures).

Standards, principles, and procedures—a basis for quality assurance in the assessment of learning

Among the many definitions of standards, principles, and procedures, we have selected the following: standards—things that are set up and established by authority for the measure of quality; principles—general or fundamental truths, comprehensive and fundamental laws, or a guide for conduct or procedures; and procedures—particular steps adopted for doing or accomplishing something.[7]

In summary, we have distinguished between the ends of instruction (the learning outcomes), the means to produce those ends (learning activities, the educational inputs), and the ways to assess the learning to ascertain the effectiveness of the learning processes. This book focuses on standards for the sound assessment of learning outcomes. These standards present specific goals as to the qualities most essential to sound assessment, along with general guidelines for pursuing and reaching those goals. In addition, practitioners are encouraged to establish effective local procedures in applying those principles. These standards, principles, and procedures together can ensure a high quality of learning assessment, whether the learning was acquired in the classroom or in the field, and whether its acquisition was teacher directed, self-directed, or undirected.

---

[7] *Webster's New World Dictionary*, ed. Victoria Neufeldt and David Guralnick (New York: Webster's New World, 1988; distributed by Prentice Hall Trade).

2 Uses and Users of Assessment Data

Educational institutions, businesses, government agencies, foundations, and professional associations are placing increasing emphasis on assessing performance in relevant areas of their domains. Growing emphasis on accountability has become a hallmark of the beginning of the twenty-first century. Consequently, a good deal of light has been cast on institutional assessment—the evaluation of how well an enterprise, as an abstracted entity, is meeting its goals. For those organizations related to education, this has meant the assessment of learning. And, though there are some distinctions, for performance evaluation in most arenas this frequently represents an assessment of learning as well.

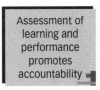

Assessment of learning and performance promotes accountability

This book focuses on assessment of learning at the level of the individual. While the strategies and principles of assessment at the organizational level are, to a great extent, parallel to assessment of individual learning, the value of the assessment processes depends foremost in the extent to which they measure and enhance a person's learning. This brings accountability a significant step closer to home so that the primary uses of assessment data lie in one or both of two categories: individual's learning and institutional or organizational credentialing.

Using Assessment to Support Learning

With the focus of assessment on individual learning, sound assessment standards and practices should be guided by a set of principles that bridge the forms of learning described in the first chapter. Assessment works best when it is a part of a person's learning process, rather than distinct from it. Because this book is directed toward assessors of higher-level learning—often equated with college-level learning, though not necessarily restricted to those institutional boundaries—adults or emerging adults of traditional college age are a reasonable population to identify as the learners of interest to us.

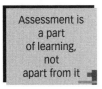

Assessment is a part of learning, not apart from it

Though discussed in the context of adult learning, the five tenets and underlying propositions in table 2.1 help describe the relationship between assessment and learning processes for learners of almost any age. They also set up the standards and principles in the chapters to follow.

Tenets of assessment and adult learning are related

TABLE 2.1

Five Tenets of Adult-Oriented Assessment and Related Propositions about Learning

■ Learning is derived from multiple sources	Their lives are complex, so adults are unlikely to have the same sources of learning as young people who have recently been in educational systems
■ Learning engages the whole person and contributes to that person's development	Learning is a critical mediator of development; maturation is the expansion of the qualities that define individual differences
■ Learning and the capacity for self-direction are promoted by feedback	Adulthood brings an expanding capacity for self-direction and self-assessment; however, both of these are capabilities that require learning and practice with feedback and can't be assumed simply by virtue of age
■ Learning occurs in context; its significance relates in part to its influence on those contexts	The contexts of which we are a part and that we create as adults become increasingly indistinguishable; among the defining features of adulthood are the kind and extent of responsibilities that adults assume and that set many of the contexts for meaningful learning
■ Learning from experiences is a unique meaning-making event that creates diversity among adults	Adults grow more unique and diverse in relation to each other; the richer the experience, the greater the potential for meaningful learning

(Adapted from Kasworm, C., & Marienau, C. (1997, Fall). Principles for assessment of adult learning. In A. Rose & M. Leahy (Eds.), *Assessing Adult Learning in Diverse Settings: Current Issues and Approaches* (pp. 5–16). San Francisco: Jossey-Bass.)

These tenets and their associated propositions point out that assessment is a series of decisions best made when guided by a set of standards, procedures, and principles, rather than an idiosyncratic moment of judgment. Depending on what aspect of learning is being examined, different assessment data are generated. In addition to assessment as a series of decisions, these tenets also suggest a set of values and a relationship between learner and assessor. The focal point is the individual learner, as the primary agent of learning, not the evaluated product of an assessment or 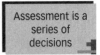 educational system. In other words, sound assessment may occur by one individual assessor, but it is much more likely to be effective in the context of a culture of assessment that both actively involves all parties and values relationships that are likely to promote learning.

Uses of Assessment Data

Both *use* and *user* serve as categories to sort data and information generated by the assessment of an individual's learning. The two umbrella categories we referred to earlier—*(a)* individual learning and *(b)* institutional or organizational credentialing—reflect the primary user of the data. The next level subcategories refer to the uses of assessment data. While each subcategory has some distinguishing features, as suggested by figure 2.1, they

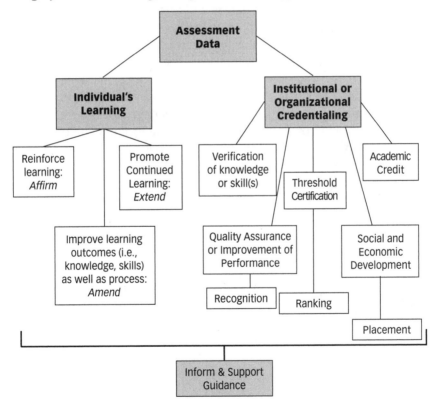

FIGURE 2.1 ■ USERS AND USES OF ASSESSMENT DATA AND INFORMATION

Individual learning and organizational credentialing are primary users of assessment data

are also closely related and often overlap. A full elaboration on each use of assessment data is beyond the scope of this book. However, practitioners should become aware of the distinctions and be clear about the intended use of the learning assessment in order to develop, apply, and communicate the appropriate expectations and strategies.

Assessment of Prior Learning

At the intersections of experiential learning/learning from experience and several use categories under the heading of "institutional or organizational credentialing" is the assessment of prior learning. Prior learning assessment (PLA) has

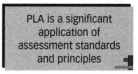

PLA is a significant application of assessment standards and principles

been receiving increased attention from a variety of sectors around the world since its emergence in the 1970s. This application of the standards and principles has a variety of names and acronyms in different countries (see Appendix A). However, its purpose is the same everywhere—the recognition of learning gained from experiences that may be granted credit or otherwise certified. This derives from a respect for adults' learning. And it is a justifiable basis for reducing redundancy and the inefficiency of requiring students to participate in one-size-fits-all curricula when they are otherwise qualified by their knowledge or skills gained from experiences.

The application of standards is most visible in the arena of PLA—or, more precisely, the assessment of learning attained through experiences irrespective of the time and place in which they occurred. Standards and principles applicable to assessing prior learning remove the centrality of teacher-directed learning and redirect attention to learning outcomes. With regard to roles, responsibilities, and capabilities of faculty, inside or outside of academia, the standards and principles shift the emphasis from teaching (input) to assessing (outcomes).

The remainder of this book is devoted to offering a foundation for assessment practitioners. It provides a set of ideas, standards and principles that apply to a wide range of contexts and have multiple uses and interpretations based on local values and purposes.

PLA can influence academic purposes and roles

CHAPTER 3

Ten Standards for Quality Assurance in Assessing Learning, Particularly for Credit or Its Equivalent

Two categories of standards are listed and discussed below pertaining to the assessment process and to quality assurance. The first five standards, pertaining to the assessment process itself, are as follows:

Standards for the assessment process

I. Credit or its equivalent should be awarded only for *learning,* and not for *experience.*

II. Assessment should be based on standards and criteria for the level of acceptable learning that are both agreed upon and made public.

III. Assessment should be treated as an integral part of learning, not apart from it, and should be based on an understanding of learning processes.

IV. The determination of credit awards and competence levels must be made by appropriate subject matter and academic or credentialing experts.

V. Credit or other credentialing should be appropriate to the context in which it is awarded and accepted.

Standards for quality assurance

The second five standards, pertaining to the administrative context in which the assessment and the award of credit occur, are as follows:

VI. If awards are for credit, transcript entries should clearly describe what learning is being recognized and be monitored to avoid giving credit twice for the same learning.

VII. Policies, procedures, and criteria applied to assessment, including provision for appeal, should be fully disclosed and prominently available to all parties involved in the assessment process.

VIII. Fees charged for assessment should be based on the services performed in the process and not determined by the amount of credit awarded.

IX. All personnel involved in the assessment of learning should pursue and receive adequate training and continuing professional development for the functions they perform.

X. Assessment programs should be regularly monitored, reviewed, evaluated, and revised as needed to reflect changes in the needs being served, the purposes being met, and in the state of the assessment arts.

The discussion that follows focuses on assessment for the purpose of awarding credit or credentialing of higher-level learning, such as college-level credit. However, all of these standards are applicable to all types of recognition of learning: waiver, advanced placement, and credit awards. Further, most of these standards are equally applicable to the assessment of learning at the secondary and postsecondary levels.

A. Academic Standards

Standard I.

Credit or its equivalent should be awarded only for *learning*, not for *experience*.

This standard is both the most important and the most frequently violated quality assurance rule in the assessment field. It is easier to quantify experience than it is to measure learning. But experience is an *input* and learning is an *outcome*; credit awards must be based on the latter.

Experience is both active and passive. It involves having thoughts, feelings, and perceptions—and acting on them. Experience concerns the discrete elements that get our attention in the everyday events of our lives. Experience is also, as John Dewey[8] described, the sum total of transactions of humans with our environment and with one another. The role of experience in forming knowledge has been the subject of extensive conversation and study by almost every discipline.

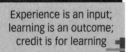

Experience is an input; learning is an outcome; credit is for learning

Unfortunately, there is no guarantee that "X" amount of experience will yield "Y" amount of learning. There are numerous variables, including individual differences among learners (e.g., biological, response to the context, personal history, cultural filters), the quality and duration of the experience, and the manner and extent to which experience is converted to

---

[8] John Dewey, *Experience and Education* (New York: Collier Books, 1938).

knowing and learning. Depending on the interaction of these variables, there may be significant learning from brief experience—and there may be little or no learning (even regression) in the wake of long and repetitive experience. In fact, as we described in chapter one, no experience is the same for all participants.

> The relationship between experience and learning differs by person and context

Two people may sit through the same lecture, one noticing a single idea and the other overwhelmed by the volume of new facts. Two potential learners put in eight hours per week at the same work station, and one may find the environment intellectually exciting and challenging while the other is baffled by the strange surroundings. Within these two situations are different experiences that ultimately yield different learning outcomes. People experience the events of their lives in different ways. Consequently, some learn more, and some less—if at all—from work, marriage, divorce, death, parenting, and other personal and social activities.

An example from traditional classroom learning amply illustrates the different ways people experience the same event. Even in the realm of classroom learning for credit, this standard may be applied unevenly. Using attendance in the determination of a course grade can result in course credit for the perfect attendee who doesn't quite get a passing grade on the assessments (e.g., examinations, papers). Conversely, some students who do get passing grades—low, but passing—may be denied credit as a result of poor attendance. Confusing experiential inputs with learning outcomes can dilute the relationship between credit and learning. Clearly, seat time, hours on the job, and life experience should not be calculated in assessing learning. They may be effective educational inputs, but they don't guarantee creditable learning outcomes.

> Confusing learning with experience per se dilutes the meaning of creditable learning

What is the value of experience? While experience may not always be a source of immediate creditable learning, it may have other essential benefits. Requiring a particular amount of experience may be reasonable for some degree or certificate programs, whether or not the experience has immediate learning results. Experience may be a platform for the application of past learning and provide effective guidance for planning future learning. It may also help one make career and personal decisions and build confidence.

In summary, experience is good for many things. One of the best things about experience is its potential as a source of learning. Learning may emerge from experience(s) reflected upon—and the range of strategies for effective reflection is remarkably extensive. But experience, by itself, is not an adequate yardstick for assessment. The most important standard for quality assurance is that credit or its equivalent is awarded for learning, and not for experience.

Standard II.

Assessment should be based on standards and criteria for the level of acceptable learning that are both agreed upon and made public.

For example, undergraduate college credit should be awarded for undergraduate-level learning, a professional credential should be awarded for learning that meets the standards of knowledge and skills of the related industry or profession, and graduate-level credit should be awarded for graduate-level learning. What, however, does a particular level of learning look like? We cannot provide an authoritative answer to this question that would satisfy every interested party. However, the question does need to be addressed by assessors of learning. The answer is a matter of discussion and debate. Ultimately, however, each institution, program, or credentialing agency or body must agree on an answer and then support and uphold it.

Levels of learning should be defined by criteria

To illustrate that *higher-level learning* can be defined in several ways, here are several different meanings or models that we have encountered. Each has distinct features but also shares some features with other meanings; others simply make one dimension or criteria more central than the others:

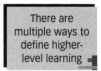
There are multiple ways to define higher-level learning

- Regarding the integration of ideas, information, theory, and application, the interplay of theory and application should be appropriate to the subject
- Reproductive knowledge that is based on current scholarly research and organized by experts
- Interpretation of one's experiences (reconstructive learning) using ideas, concepts, and analogies from one or more disciplines or domains and/or supported ideas or theories of one's own
- Skills or abilities that represent an interplay of at least two of the following domains of learning: abstract, analytic, and/or creative thinking; nuanced perception; complex behaviors; emotional breadth
- A listing in a college catalog[9]

---

[9] This definition is worthy of a few comments because of its common usage. Unfortunately, catalog listings are often not a reliable guide for identifying college-level learning. In some respects they are too restrictive, and in other respects not restrictive enough. Rarely explicit

- Any combination of the above and other criteria at the discretion or judgment of designated experts (e.g., faculty) in the assessor's role.

Each of these expressions draws upon the categories of depth, breadth, and complexity to define higher-level (e.g., college-level) learning. Distinctions between undergraduate, graduate, or professional levels would require further differentiation. As exclusive sources of learning, both the traditional and experiential modes have predictable weaknesses. The common observation about classroom-bound learners is that, although they may have scored high on examinations about theory, they are weak when it comes to actual application. The common observation about experiential learners is that often they can do (in a particular setting) but can't explain—because they haven't really mastered the general principles that would allow them to apply their learning in new settings or the language to discuss the concepts embodying those principles in an analytic way.

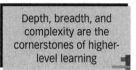

Depth, breadth, and complexity are the cornerstones of higher-level learning

In some subject areas—for example, teaching and medicine—there is a reasonably clear distinction between the theory needs and the applied learning needs. In others—history, for example—it is more difficult to divide the learning on the basis of theory and practice. Consequently, different models or definitions of higher-level learning may be necessary, depending on the context, rather than a one-size-fits-all approach. In other words, everyone must exhibit a balance between theory and practice.

Finally, a word of caution about the role of experts in defining this standard: While the expertise of faculties is essential to the successful application of the standard in the college context, that expertise alone does not provide automatic quality assurance. The expansion of experiential learning programs exposes a serious double standard. Significant criticism has

about the basis for their designation as creditworthy, they can be less than reliable guides to identify the level of learner competence that qualifies for college credit. It may be relatively easy to gauge college-level competence in a subject like mathematics, but more difficult for some of the social sciences and humanities. Even with mathematics, however, there is overlap both in content and mastery between high school and college. With foreign language, the confusion can be more serious. What are the distinctions, if any, between high school Spanish 4 and College Spanish 1? How should we respond to a high school student in Mexico who may have language mastery superior to that of a two- or three-term college student of Spanish in the United States? And how do we view a speaking knowledge of a language that is not in our local catalog but might be college-accredited elsewhere. Using catalogs as the standard can limit the flexibility needed in some cases to serve legitimate individual needs. And, in fact, not all catalog listings are acceptable by consensus among colleges as identifying work of college level.

been levelled by traditionalists against experiential learning programs, particularly in PLA, alleging that they fail to require a theoretical balance to qualify for college credit. The complaint is often legitimate. Conversely, the A students in an accounting class, for example, may not have all the learning necessary to apply the classroom knowledge in the workplace as successfully as they can pass exams on it in the classroom. These are vitally important issues in the assessment of experiential learning, and they are just as vital in the awarding of credit for theoretical courses. The double standard can mask serious weaknesses in a curriculum where unbalanced credit awards are more prevalent for theory courses than for internships or PLAs. This standard of making public the standards and criteria for the level of acceptable learning arises for just that reason.

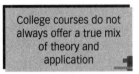

College courses do not always offer a true mix of theory and application

This standard is vital to the assessment of learning for credit or credentialing. But meeting the requirements of this standard necessarily entails judgment and subjectivity—hence, the need for discussion, agreement, and periodic revision among those adopting and applying the standard. Various principles of good practice derived from other standards in this set will reinforce quality assurance in applying this standard.

Standard III.

Assessment should be treated as an integral part of learning, not separate from it, and should be based on an understanding of learning processes.

This standard embraces two ideas:

- Assessment should be a measurement, not an audit, of learning.
- How assessment is done is an outgrowth of beliefs and assumptions about learning.

What ties together these ideas is the belief that *(a)* a primary purpose of assessment is to inform and guide learning (figure 2.1), and *(b)* essentially every model of learning posits a role for assessment—and feedback—as part of the process.

Assessment is an integral part of learning

There are a variety of ways to make assessment an integral part of learning—make it frequent, use a blend of formative and summative assessment events, employ sound feedback practices, and ensure assessment methods are valid (i.e., they measure what they are intended to measure), and measure what matters. Additionally, assessment is more likely to be experienced as a part of learning when it is *(a)* based on criteria that are clearly expressed and known to both the assessor and the learner, and *(b)* presented in ways that are likely to be read or heard by the learner as constructive and useful for a future learning agenda if one is desired. Assessments can take the form of audits, as in a result of pass/fail, a test score, a proportion of successful behaviors relative to attempts, or a grade. While these audits may communicate assessment judgments or data from the perspective of the institutional or credentialing agency, they are not embedded in or experienced as a part of a learning process.

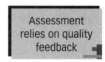

Assessment relies on quality feedback

Even when assessment is intentionally made part of a learning process, differing beliefs or assumptions can influence what model or theory of learning is adopted; these, in turn, can affect how well this standard is met. If, for example, the model of learning is that relative novices learn most effectively and efficiently by primarily listening to or imitating an expert, then the assessment may take the form of an evaluation of how well the student retained the information or can reproduce the expert's knowledge. If the conception of learning behind this approach also accounts for how retention of information may be promoted, then the assessment might also provide feedback on patterns of errors, if there are any, to focus attention for improvement in retention.

Or, if the model of learning posits that much of what may be learned from experiences remains tacit until prompted, the assessment should be constructed to provide relevant or stimulating prompts. This phase may require considerable care and patience to avoid preempting the demonstration of the learning outcomes.

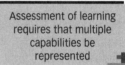

Assessment of learning requires that multiple capabilities be represented

We are intentionally avoiding naming or advocating specific models or theories of learning—the literature is too vast and complex to do it justice in a brief overview. However, even these few examples illustrate the importance of this standard as a component of good assessment practice.

Standard IV.

The determination of credit awards and competence levels must be made by appropriate subject matter and academic or credentialing experts.

The consensus of experts is probably the most effective mechanism for maintaining adequate standards. Even with Standard II in place—or perhaps because of it—credit awards depend on the judgment of faculty or organizationally appointed experts.

Two kinds of expertise should be brought to bear on decisions about credit. One is content expertise: How much does the learner know, and how well does she/he know it? The other is academic or credentialing expertise: Given the extent and quality of the learning, is college credit or credentialing appropriate? If so, how much, in what subject(s), at what level, and with or without the completion of additional learning?

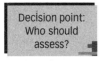

Two kinds of expertise should be involved in determining creditworthy learning

Ideally, these aspects of expertise would be combined to be most efficient. One of the decisions a program or agency must make is how to answer the question "Who can or should assess?" For example, when assessing learning for college credit, the subject matter may be deemed appropriate for college credit but is not included in the particular college's curriculum. In this case, it may be necessary to consult outside content experts while preserving the credit decision for local academic determination. This is one of those decision points: Are only subjects represented in a curriculum appropriate for credit? Are only local faculty appropriate to assess? A shared decision, for example, may include input from outside content experts on the level of learning and local academic experts on the amount of credit. This approach could preserve quality assurance while extending the institution's flexibility and range. In some ways it is similar to the extended range of service that one campus enjoys when it accepts transfer credit from other accredited institutions in subjects not locally taught. It is also the principle that permits colleges and universities to grant credit for The College Level Examination Program (CLEP), DANTES, or American Council on Education (ACE)—approved assessments of noncampus learning whether or not the credited subject is taught on the campus. The standard applies, however, no matter how the decision is made regarding who is appropriate to assess.

Decision point: Who should assess?

Standard V.

Credit or other credentialing should be appropriate to the context in which it is awarded and accepted.

There are several factors that can create the context referred to in this standard—for example, a curriculum, personal goals, professional standards, and regulations. Each of these should be considered when determining the relevance and creditability of learning. One or the other factors will usually take precedence, but the standard is most effective when all relevant factors are included in the judgment.

This rule is applicable to all learning, regardless of its sources. Limiting credit for experiential learning only to certain aspects of the learner's program is to apply a double standard. College-creditable experiential learning occurs in the major, in general education, and in electives. Professional-level capabilities may be the outcome of learning from multiple experiences in a range of applied contexts. Provided that college credit is awarded only for learning that meets the criteria for higher-level learning (Standards I and II) in the judgment of qualified content and academic or credentialing experts (Standard IV), the adequacy of program fit should be determined independently of the source of the learning.

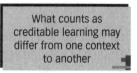
What counts as creditable learning may differ from one context to another

There are two reasons why particular care may be needed in fitting experiential learning to the credentialing or certification contexts. First, experiential learning is often idiosyncratic and usually defies a straightforward connection to a course catalog, structured training program, or standardized test description. Second, in the case of transfer credit, there may be significant differences in how different institutions determine what learning fits which degree or certificate.

B. Administrative Standards

Standard VI.

If awards are for credit, transcript entries should clearly describe what learning is being recognized and should be monitored to avoid giving credit twice for the same learning.

In one respect, meeting this standard is a simple administrative matter. However, it may require academic judgment in cases where the relationships of the subject matter are complex or where credited learning has not been adequately described or clearly labeled. In any case, it is a decision that should be made before learning such as through traditional courses or internships is undertaken, or in the case of prior learning, before learning is assessed and credited. For that reason, it should be a scheduled item in the assessment process.

Duplication of credit should be avoided

Traditional titles for credited components often are not accurate descriptions of the individual learning outcomes of a particular idiosyncratic input. In such cases, where generally understood labels would not fully reflect the true nature of the credited learning content, it is necessary to clearly define and properly label the learning. This is crucial both for the evaluating institution and in the event of transfer of credit between institutions. In the case of college courses, a course catalog description may not be available for such idiosyncratic learning components; thus, the original transcribing institution needs to make clear the nature of the learning so that appropriate decisions can be made about potential duplication, overlap, and program fit. When transcribing courses, decisions ensuring against duplication are usually made in advance and built into the academic regulations. For PLA, such clarifications and specifications need to be explicitly monitored to ensure consistency with standard registrar practice.

Standard VII.

Policies, procedures, and criteria applied to assessment, including provision for appeal, should be fully disclosed and prominently available to all parties involved in the assessment process.

"Truth in advertising" is a vital component of quality assurance. Learners, accrediting agencies, other institutions, and the consumer public should know what rules are applied in learning assessment. Making visible the application of the other standards here should make this standard mostly just a matter of good communication. However, it may also be a matter of local culture that makes this standard more or less easy to enforce; for example, the extent to which Standard III is incorporated into policy and practices may vary, depending on whether it is deemed important to make assessment criteria available to stakeholders in the process.

> Policies and practices should be publicly available to ensure equity

It is important that the rules be comprehensive, explicit, and accessible. Every caution should be taken to avoid misleading statements that encourage unrealistic expectations.

Standard VIII.

Fees charged for assessment should be based on the services performed in the process and not determined by the amount of credit awarded.

In traditional programs, the cost of instruction, including assessment, is the same whether the student passes the course and is awarded credit, or fails and receives no credit. This relationship between fees and credit must be replicated in programs to assess experiential learning in order to preserve quality. Based on the rationale that the time and

> Fees should only be charged for assessment, not for credit

effort by assessors is likely to vary with the complexity of the presented evidence of learning, fees may vary as the amount of credit attempted varies. But because of the potential for creating an appearance of credit for a fee, fees must not be based solely on the amount of credit awarded.

The distinction between fee-for-credit and fee-for-assessment is especially important when prior or independent learning is assessed for a course equivalency. In this case, the basis for any fees should be the assessment itself as well as associated administrative costs, not the tuition cost of the credit hours that are awarded.

Standard IX.

All personnel involved in the assessment of learning should pursue and receive adequate training and continuing professional development for the functions they perform.

This standard poses a reciprocal responsibility for both assessors and institutions/organizations/agencies that provide and support learning assessment. The standard is as necessary for classroom teachers and assessors as it is for experiential learning personnel. Maintaining the effectiveness of the entire set of standards rests on both *(a)* the desire of assessors (e.g., faculty, performance evaluators) to assume knowledge-based responsibility for their efforts, and *(b)* the intention of organizations they represent to provide sustained training along with assessment of the quality of the frontline assessors' work.

It has often been noted that college and university professors are better prepared in content than they are in process. Most advanced degree programs tend to prepare students for research. It might fairly be argued that most college and university faculty have had virtually no preparation for their teaching and assessment roles, whether performed in traditional settings or for experiential learning. Even  for those who have developed appropriate assessment expertise for classroom learning (usually through self-directed experiential learning), it is essential that professional development be sought and provided in support of any experiential learning assessment they undertake.

Professional development is a reciprocal responsibility

Standard X.

Assessment programs should be monitored, reviewed, evaluated, and revised as needed to reflect changes in the needs being served, the purposes being met, and in the state of the assessment arts.

Local review and evaluation can take various formal and informal forms, including internal self-study and assessment and involvement of outside advisory panels. One of the keys to upholding this standard is to periodically revisit the purpose(s) and role(s) of assessment activities (see figure 2.1). Accrediting agencies and professional associations can partner with national organizations that offer assistance for monitoring programs and assuring quality, such as The Council for Adult and Experiential Learning (CAEL). The more often systems for monitoring quality are embedded in local assessment activities, the more likely it is that this standard will be met in an unobtrusive manner.

> Assessment programs require periodic comprehensive review to build quality

Prologue to Chapters 4 and 5

The standards described in chapter 3 are met in different ways by different institutions. Depending on the organizational mission and on the personal goals of the learners, different institutions may establish their own unique policies to meet the standards described in chapter 3. However, there are

> Principles and procedures for assessing learning differ for sponsored and unsponsored learning

certain general principles of good practice that every institution should follow in order to achieve a standard of excellence in assessment.

Principles and procedures for assessing learning differ significantly depending on whether the learning is planned and sponsored—for instance, by an organization such as a postsecondary institution or a performance development group—or is unsponsored prior learning that is often the unplanned result of work and other life experiences (i.e., experiential learning).

Under the umbrella of sponsored learning, there are several categories representing varying methods of assessment. For example, sponsored learning includes credit-bearing courses, non-credit-bearing classes or workshops, and planned experiential learning events. Sponsored learning certainly may take other forms, but the primary characteristic is that the learning event is *"pre-planned" planning*, at least primarily, by somebody other than the learner(s). Under the umbrella of sponsored learning, there may be considerable differences in how assessment of learning or performance is included in the planning and realization of the learning event(s), if it is, in fact, included. The institutions may also differ in how they convert the assessment into credit or a credential for public representation. Credit-bearing courses have—almost by definition—an assessment component in order to determine if someone has earned the credit. Noncredit, sponsored learning events may or may not contain an assessment component.

The type of learning of most interest here is experiential. The most important difference between sponsored and unsponsored types of experiential learning is that the former has the advantages of preplanning. Both the specific learning objectives and the selection of appropriate learning activities can be planned in advance. In addition, the measurement and evaluation of the learning can be incorporated into the learning process, although it may not be. In credit-granting or credentialing situations, unsponsored experiential learning is clearly the object of assessment activities that are represented by the general phrase "prior learning assessment."

These important differences in assessment considerations for sponsored and unsponsored (prior learning) assessment have led us to treat them separately as we move from a discussion of standards (equally applicable to the two sources of learning) and begin a discussion of the principles and procedures that facilitate the maintenance of those standards. In chapter 4, we will discuss the principles and procedures for assessing *sponsored* experiential learning. In chapter 5, we will discuss the principles and procedures for assessing *prior* experiential learning. Ultimately, however, the distinctions between sponsored and unsponsored learning are only important insofar as they are useful for determining what a student brings to the table to be assessed for credit or credentialing and for the formation of policies and practices that assure the quality of assessment.

> The distinctions between sponsored and unsponsored learning are only as useful as the practices they inform

The assessment components of both types of learning follow six steps. These steps do not have to be completed in a particular order. Step 6, *transcription*, for example, is the last step in both sponsored and unsponsored learning assessment (see table 4.1). And while sponsored learning assessment involves setting learning objectives and outcomes at the outset, unsponsored PLA does not. Similarly, the *documentation* step in sponsored learning can be planned as an integral part of the *measurement* step, while in PLA, documentation usually occurs after the learning itself.

> Though there are six steps in the assessment of both sponsored and unsponsored learning, the order of comparable steps may differ considerably

In some respects, *evaluation* (i.e., the determination of credit amounts, grades, certification) is the last step before *transcription* in the assessment of either prior unsponsored or sponsored learning. However, in most instances of sponsored learning, a significant part of the *evaluation* is done provisionally before the learning takes place. For example, most internship or community-based courses in colleges have projected credit values. Evaluation at the end is primarily to confirm (or deny) the satisfactory completion of learning objectives set at the beginning of the course along with judgment as to the relative quality of the learning outcomes, which is how grades are assigned. Evaluation for credentialing may result in a judgment of the relative quality of the learning outcomes as a "value-added" component (consistent with Standard III) in addition to the basic determination of whether a threshold level of competence has been achieved.

The results of the assessment process may also influence the process itself. Unintended outcomes, in the case of sponsored learning, and unsuspected or previously tacit (and therefore possibly unclaimed) outcomes, in the case of prior learning, may alter the amount or type of credit that is appropriate. For systems with sufficient flexibility, this is particularly important in the case of sponsored learning, as it may necessitate changes in the amount of credit that was projected for service learning, an internship, or another experiential learning activity. The fifth step, *measurement*, may thus lead to revision of the third step, *provisional evaluation*. The assessment process may not proceed exactly in the order it appears in this book. What is important is recognizing that interrelationships exist among the six steps and finding ways to work with them in a system.

Ideally, assessment processes should be both dynamic and an important source of new learning and new insights about personal and professional goals. A rigid, mechanistic approach to the process should be avoided. Each of the six steps is an important component, but the order in which they are accomplished may vary with individual circumstances. Therefore, a practical approach is to view the six steps as a checklist, leaving the question of order open to continuous review and cross-checking.

Principles and Procedures for Assessing Sponsored Learning

Table 4.1 lists the six components of assessment associated with sponsored learning situations and the standard that guides each component. As already noted, there are six steps to a full assessment process. However, they may or may not all be included in any given learning event. The conditions for including or excluding any of the steps are noted in the table. The decision to include or exclude is dependent on at least two factors: whether credit or credentialing is awarded, and how much attention the sponsoring body or individual teacher chooses to give to assessment. The steps involved in assessing sponsored learning apply equally well to teacher-directed or experiential learning; the latter, however, will be the primary focus of most of the information on the six steps that constitute a sound assessment process in the sponsored learning context.

TABLE 4.1		
The Assessment of Sponsored Experiential Learning		
STEPS	**ALWAYS INCLUDED?**	**RELEVANT STANDARD(S)**
1. Articulation Relate learning goals to academic, professional, or personal goals	Yes	*Standard V* Credit or other credentialing should be appropriate to the context in which it is awarded and accepted.
2. Planning Select appropriate learning objectives and activities	Yes	*Standard I* Credit or its equivalent should be awarded only for learning, and not for experience.
		Standard II Assessment should be based on standards and criteria for the level of acceptable learning that are both agreed upon and made public.

(continued)

TABLE 4.1

STEPS	ALWAYS INCLUDED?	RELEVANT STANDARD(S)
2. Planning *(continued)*		*Standard III* Assessment should be treated as an integral part of learning, not separate from it, and should be based on an understanding of learning processes.
3. Evaluation Determine the credit equivalency	Yes, if learning outcomes are measured and credit or credential is to be awarded	*Standard IV* The determination of credit awards and competence levels must be made by appropriate subject matter and academic or credentialing experts.
4. Documentation Collect or create evidence of learning	Yes, if learning outcomes are measured and credit or credential is to be awarded Yes, if learning outcomes are measured but credit/credential is not awarded Optional if learning is neither measured nor credit/credential awarded	*Standard I* Credit or its equivalent should be awarded only for learning, and not for experience. *Standard II* Assessment should be based on standards and criteria for the level of acceptable learning that are both agreed upon and made public. *Standard III* Assessment should be treated as an integral part of learning, not separate from it, and should be based on an understanding of learning processes. *Standard IV* The determination of credit awards and competence levels must be made by appropriate subject matter and academic or credentialing experts.
5. Measurement Determine the degree and level of competence/ learning achieved	Yes, if credit/ credential is awarded	*Standard II* Assessment should be based on standards and criteria for the level of acceptable learning that are both agreed upon and made public.

(continued)

TABLE 4.1

The Assessment of Sponsored Experiential Learning (CONTINUED)

STEPS	ALWAYS INCLUDED?	RELEVANT STANDARD(S)
5. Measurement *(continued)*	May not be in noncredit or noncredentialing situations	*Standard III* Assessment should be treated as an integral part of learning, not apart from it, and should be based on an understanding of learning processes.
6. Transcription Prepare a useful record of results	Yes, if learning is measured and credit or credential awarded Optional if learning is neither measured nor awarded credit/ credential	*Standard VI* If awards are for credit, transcript entries should clearly describe what learning is being recognized and be monitored to avoid giving credit twice for the same learning.

The first two steps in the assessment of sponsored experiential learning are, in essence, the development of a learning plan that may be constructed with an individual or organized for a group. If individualized, step 1 entails review of a learner's goals—short- or long-term—and sets the context for learning in relation to the sponsoring organization's purposes, capacities, or requirements (Standard V). When the articulation and planning are individualized, the learner may benefit from some advising or coaching assistance by a faculty member or comparable support person. If a group is involved, step 1 entails consideration of the collective needs or interests and their relationship to the sponsoring organization's purpose, capabilities, and requirements, particularly if this plan will be leading to academic credit or other credentialing.

Step 2 moves from an articulation of appropriate goals to the identification of specific learning objectives and outcomes. The determination of learning activities to achieve the outcomes follows this identification. At this point in the planning process, Standards I, II, and III are reviewed to ensure that the experiential activities can lead to learning that will meet a designated set of standards and have an assessment component built into the process.[10]

Step 3, evaluation, may not always fit intuitively into the planned assessment process at this point. But it is the point at which we determine the amount of credit or level of credentialing that may be awarded if the learning objectives of step 2 are met satisfactorily. Standard IV presents guidelines for determining who makes this decision. The credit is provisional—in other words, the actual award of credit is contingent on satisfactory completion of the planned learning. This step must be reviewed at the end of the process after the appropriate assessor (e.g., faculty member, credentialing expert) has measured the learning outcomes (step 5).

Step 4, documentation, is the production or collection of evidence that proves the learning objectives have been met. The success of this step is usually facilitated by advance arrangements with the assessor. In accordance with Standard III, an assessor provides ongoing feedback on both the learning and the effectiveness of the documentation in providing evidence that the learning satisfies the requirements of Standards I and II.

Step 5, measurement of learning outcomes, is the culmination of the assessment process. It is, per Standard IV, a responsibility of an appropriate expert (e.g., faculty member). It also is a concluding exercise of Standard III, providing feedback and judging, if the system is flexible enough. At this point, the assessor should determine whether the provisional credit projected in step 3 has, in fact, been earned.

Evaluators also should consider whether some unintended (and possibly creditable) learning has also occurred. A full evaluation of planned future learning may reveal changes in personal or professional goals as a result of the recent learning experiences. Finally, it is in step 5 that the assessor needs to anticipate any necessary inputs for the transcribing process, step 6.

Step 6, transcribing the results, is primarily an administrative responsibility. In the case of scheduled experiential learning events—such as community-based activities, internships, or other regularly offered field-experience courses—the process may be fairly routine, much like the completion of any catalog course. A question of duplicated credit (Standard VI) may

---

[10] Before addressing the remaining steps, we should point out that we have not included a discussion of the interplay between these steps and learning processes themselves—in other words, in the midst of a sponsored experiential learning event, any number of strategies can help people learn from their experiences, including feedback and assessment. While a discussion of these strategies is beyond the scope of this book, we also realize that its exclusion here is inconsistent with Standard III, which deals with treating assessment as an integral part of learning, not apart from it.

also arise if significant unintended learning outcomes emerge, though these are not likely to supercede the intended outcomes in terms of measured learning. However, the assessor should be aware of the question of duplicated credit and provide any information that may be needed for accurate transcription.

The rest of this chapter is devoted to the principles and procedures that support the ten standards of quality assurance. The principles and procedures are also summarized in checklist form in Appendix B.

Steps, Principles, and Procedures

Step 1. ARTICULATION
Relate learning goals to academic, personal, and professional goals.

The basis for granting college credit does not rest on one particular standard, such as college level. In most instances, the validity of counting learning for credit depends upon a demonstrable relationship to a defined degree or other program or course objectives. This step is particularly important in the initial planning of a curriculum and in individualized degree programs. In this first step, then, we will consider principles and procedures that relate to the two standards of quality assurance: *(a)* that the learning fits the context in which the credit or credential is being awarded and *(b)* that the determination of the level of learning meets an acceptable standard (Standard II).

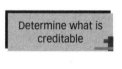

Determine what is creditable

1.1 Each institution or organization should have a published rationale for crediting particular types of learning in each of its programs or offerings. As program requirements respond to changes in society or professions and seek to serve unique needs of individual learners, institutions should have published processes for making exceptions as well as extending or changing the rationale for determining what is creditable.

Define criteria for acceptable standards of learning

1.2 There should be an institutional explanation of the criteria for determining the standards of a desired level of learning (Standard II).

1.3 Learner and institution/organization should reach a clear understanding as to the general learning activity and the connection between personal or professional goals and the degree, course, or credential requirements.

| Define learner's rationale or general reason(s) for seeking the learning objectives | **1.31** Use this opportunity to help individuals understand and choose learning goals that enhance self-awareness and personal development.

1.32 Students should be encouraged to negotiate new or different learning objectives if their experience so warrants. Sponsored learning activities combine the necessity for increased learner responsibility with the opportunity to develop the skills of self-managed learning and assessment. |

| To the extent possible, coordinate goals with the learning environment | **1.4** For internships, field placements, on-the-job, and community-based learning activities, care should be taken to match the learning environment to goals. Students should have enough information to understand the pros and cons of alternate field placements in relation to learning objectives. |

Step 2. PLANNING

Select appropriate learning objectives and activities.

Standard I dictates that only learning, not experience, should be credited. Standard II requires that only learning that meets agreed-upon standards and criteria should be granted credit by colleges and universities. These quality assurance criteria are more likely to be satisfied if careful attention is given to the planning of specific learning objectives that clearly differentiate between the experiential inputs and the learning outcomes. An important principle that helps to assure good practice, for example, is that field experience learning should not be undertaken without adequate preparation of the student and anyone on the field side who will be guiding the student.

| Determine the standards and associated criteria for the acceptable level of learning | **2.1** Determining the standards that represent an acceptable level of learning requires considerable discussion, evaluation of others' ideas, and reiterative review of agreements. A variety of components are often considered in these deliberations: |

(a) demonstrate a conceptual as well as a practical grasp of the knowledge or competence acquired;

(b) have learning that is relevant to contexts in addition to the specific context in which it was acquired;

(c) acquire learning that falls within the domain usually considered appropriate to college credit as represented in the catalogs and practices of the colleges and universities.

Other considerations may and should go into the deliberations toward agreements that are germane to the particular institution or organization.

**Develop a
learning plan**

2.2 To support the achievement of Standard I (credit learning, not experience), the learning plan should clearly differentiate between the experiential inputs and the creditable learning outcomes.

2.21 Learning outcomes should be expressed as specifically as possible in terms of the competences (knowledge or skills) to be achieved. This should be separated from other components of the planning (e.g., the description of the level of competence and the process by which it will be evaluated and measured). (See Steps 3 and 5.)

2.22 Learning activities should be selected and planned for each learning objective and in anticipation of the evaluation and measurement steps in the assessment process. (See Principle 2.4 on learning contracts.) Among the most important of the learning activities is formative evaluation (Standard III). Periodic reflection to check on progress helps to avoid unanticipated dead ends and to make any needed changes in the learning plan. Both the teacher and the learner should be alert to the real possibility that some unintended, but useful, learning may occur. Thus, assessment at the end of the planned learning should also consider unexpected learning results that may be quite different from—and possibly even better than—the intended learning.

2.23 In finding the most effective fit between the intended outcomes and the selection of experiential activities, the learner's strategies and styles of learning—describable by a variety of models as well as measures—might well be ascertained and taken into account in terms of *planning toward congruence* or *planning toward stretching*.

**Emphasize
learner's role in
preparing for a
sponsored
experiential
learning**

2.3 The learning process is enhanced when the learner is required to assume significant responsibility for it. Applying this principle increases the likelihood of heightened self-awareness and confidence and a more effective relationship between what has been learned in the past and what future learning is planned.

2.31 The learning activities are likely to be enhanced if the planning includes an orientation to the specific learning environment. Both formative and summative evaluations are also enhanced by continuation of a process initiated through an orientation process.

**Bridge the planning
and evaluation
steps: learning
contracts**

2.4 One means of bridging the planning and evaluation steps is through a written learning contract. This helps the learner and evaluator/assessor reach an understanding as to the kinds and levels of learning outcomes and how they will be evaluated.

Step 3. EVALUATION
Determine the credit equivalency.

Evaluating (Does it meet college-creditable standards?) and measuring (How much has been learned and at what level?) learning are two vitally important steps in the assessment process. When assessing prior learning it is necessary to first measure and then evaluate. For planned learning, however, it is useful to evaluate first (i.e., to describe the type and degree of competence that qualifies for a certain amount of credit) before the parties—learner, sponsor, and field personnel—accept a specified commitment. This third step, evaluation, will need to be reviewed after completion of the fifth step, measurement, to determine whether the measured learning has met the test for the credit. A sponsored experiential learning event is organized in much the same way as a typical classroom situation: The amount of credit for the course is specified in advance, learning outcomes are (or should be) articulated, and the measurement (e.g., final exams, term papers, etc.) is applied at the end to determine whether the learning outcomes have met the test for credit.

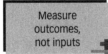

Decide who categorizes and defines competencies

3.1 Institutional policy concerning the standard-setting authority should be clear. Individual institutions decide how standards are to be set. Standards may be defined on the basis of institutional program objectives, the objectives of students, or the requirements of third parties (occupational or educational). It is normally desirable to take all three into account. (See also Principle 2.1.)

Define evaluation criteria and make them public

3.2 In evaluating any learning plan, establish as early as practicable the standards that will be used as a basis for awarding credit (including grades) or a credential. Measure the individuals learning by these standards.

3.21 Use clear criteria and examples to show different levels of competence. This way, different people can receive different levels of competence.

Measure outcomes, not inputs

3.3 Assessment of experiential learning should place emphasis upon criterion-referenced assessment so that individuals are evaluated in terms of expected learning outcomes, not on time on task or activity. (Standard I).

3.4 Standards for crediting or recognizing experiential learning should be the same as, or comparable to, standards for crediting or recognizing learning by other means.

3.41 The basis for translating outcomes into credit hours or credential thresholds should be specified. Time spent on an activity should not be a primary consideration in determining credit or credential equivalency.

There are several approaches to connecting learning outcomes with credit or credit equivalencies—for example, credit hour equivalencies can be established for particular accomplishments, or learning outcomes can be matched with those of existing courses. Equivalent academic hours may be estimated to help predict what learning activities will be necessary but should not be relied on for direct translation of experience into learning for credit or its equivalent. Formal guidelines help ensure equity in awards.

3.5 Evaluation (determining relationship of learning to credit/credentialing and grades) and measurement (determining depth and level of learning) should be formative (providing feedback during the process) as well as summative (making judgments, drawing conclusions at the end of the process) (Standard III).

3.51 A review of prior learning should precede each new learning activity and relate it to the learner's objective.

3.52 Feedback should be offered during the learning activity(ies) to monitor progress toward the intended outcomes and to prompt any changes in either objectives or activities.

3.53 Summative feedback should be provided as soon as possible after the completion of the learning activity. It should include an explanation of credit or credential awards and implications for program or degree requirements. The summative evaluation should also serve as the initial step in planning future learning (Principle 3.51).

Step 4. DOCUMENTATION
Create and organize evidence of learning.

The presentation of adequate evidence of learning is an important step in assessment. Such documentation comes in many forms, and different types of documentation serve different functions and have different characteristics. The primary purpose of any documentation should be to illustrate what someone has learned. It may be supported by personal verification from a qualified assessor external to the organization or institution, such as a site supervisor.

Develop an institutional policy(ies)

4.1 Institutions/organizations should formulate a clear policy as to what types of learning require documentation and what function the documentation is intended to serve.

Documentation may serve several distinguishable functions: *(a)* organizing proper documentation may in itself be a useful learning strategy even if it serves no administrative purpose; *(b)* documentation can be viewed as an accumulation of information useful in assessment on a formative basis (including a source or memory for self-assessment) as well as a summative one; *(c)* documentation can be seen largely as a means of consulting third-party expertise; and *(d)* documentation can serve simply as a useful record (for either the institution or student).

Specify appropriate documentation

4.2 There should be clear institutional/organizational specifications as to what types of documentation are appropriate for what types of learning.

Examples of different types of documentation should be available, along with descriptions of the functions they serve and how they should be solicited and presented. Types of documentation include, but are not limited to the following:

a) testimony regarding competence; *(b)* learning products (e.g., essays, work samples, learning logs); *(c)* performance or examinations, oral or written; and *(d)* demonstrations or simulations.

4.21 Guidelines for documentation should make clear in what ways documentation provided by the student might be used in assessment.

Documentation should distinguish experience from learning

4.3 Care should be taken in determining whether particular documentation describes experience or provides evidence of learning.

4.31 Descriptions of a learning activity may or may not constitute evidence of learning. In some instances, documentation of participation in an activity may constitute adequate evidence of learning. This can occur when participation is contingent upon having mastered certain competencies or qualifications. In this case, the screening or testing associated with the activity serves as a surrogate assessment process. Entry into certain civil service jobs or professional certifications, for example, requires demonstration of particular competencies. If certificates or similar documentation are taken as evidence of specific competences, it must be clear that there has been an assessment of learning or performance and that the criteria on which this assessment was based is consistent with criteria for an acceptable level of learning (Standard II).

Authenticate and qualify evidence

4.4 Assessors should take all reasonable and necessary steps to ensure that evidence of learning is accurate and that the student is, in fact, responsible for evidence presented. There should be public guidelines as to what constitutes authentic documentation.

4.41 Authentication procedures for evidence transmitted electronically or through Internet-based interactions are still evolving. Procedures for authentication should incorporate appropriate technology and reflect decisions regarding the message concerning trust that an institution or organization wants to communicate through its language, policies, and procedures.

4.42 When documenting learning by testimony, procedures for obtaining letters should clarify the nature of the learning and the dependability of the source of evidence.

The credentials of individuals writing letters in support of student learning should be clear. Individuals writing such letters should know the student and have firsthand knowledge of the experiential learning cited. A documentation letter should state the nature of the author's relationship to the student as well as the author's credentials as an expert judge (Standard IV); otherwise, evidence of a conflict of interest or bias may be overlooked. If appropriate, the letter should be written on official stationery.

4.43 Either the student or the assessor—or both—should make it clear to those providing documentation that they are being asked only to provide evidence of the level and depth of learning, not a recommendation of credit, grading, or credentialing.

Judge quality, not quantity

4.5 Care must be exercised to ensure that the quantity and the attractiveness of the presentation of evidence do not influence the award of credit or its equivalent. Credit awards must be based on learning, not experience (Standard I) and on accurate measurement of the quality and depth of learning at the desired level (Standard II). (See also Step 5, below.)

Step 5. MEASUREMENT
Determine the degree and level of learning/competence achieved.

This step in assessment involves determining the extent and character of the knowledge or skill acquired. The principles and procedures that are followed in this part of the process will support the achievement of several of the ten standards. Perhaps most important, these principles and procedures are clearly related to Standard IV (ensuring that competency judgments are made by qualified experts), and Standard III (the integration of assessment into the learning process), and also have a close relationship with Standard IX (the importance of adequately training assessors). Accuracy of judgment is particularly essential since inconsistency from one judge to another is unfair to students and may discredit the assessment process. Quality assurance depends on both the reliability (Principle 5.4) and validity (Principle 5.5) of the measurement process.

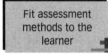

5.1 Assessment of learning—whether experiential or teacher directed—should employ measurement methods that fit the character of the learning and the outcomes intended to be measured. Intentions to measure reconstructive learning outcomes should not be measured by strategies or techniques that elicit data regarding reproductive learning and vice versa.

Assessment strategies may incorporate standardized testing, but it should not be the only method. Much experiential learning is characterized by different learning outcomes for different individuals and, thus, may require differing assessment strategies from person to person to person.

5.2 In measuring an individual's learning, assessors should use techniques that are appropriate to the background and characteristics of the learner. Methods should take into account individual differences among people, including limitations associated with disabilities.

5.3 Assessment should be a useful learning experience in itself and construed as part of the overall learning event (Standard III).

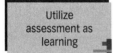

The best assessment strategies create opportunities for additional learning as well as measurement of what has already been learned. Assessment goals should be reflected in learning activities, and learners should be included in the assessment process. An appreciation of the purpose of assessment can help reinforce an individual's responsibility for her/his own learning and create a sense of mutual accountability with the assessor.

Improved self-awareness and better understanding of the techniques of self-assessment are in themselves learning outcomes of assessment. Thus, the greater extent to which assessment is experienced as a mix of instruction, evaluation, and measurement of learning, the greater the likelihood that self-managed learning can be developed. Both the formative and summative stages of evaluative measurement offer opportunities to develop this outcome.

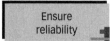

Ensure reliability

5.4 Institutions should strive for assessment that is as reliable (i.e., consistent) as possible in order to ensure fairness to students.

5.41 To improve consistency in assessment judgments, more than one sample of learning should be examined whenever possible.

5.42 Unless there is evidence that one assessor is sufficient or financial constraints are prohibitive, more than one assessor should be used. Judgments of different assessors can vary considerably and systematically if they have had limited experience from which to learn or if assessment guidelines are not clear.

5.43 Assessors should strive to avoid bias, discrimination, or unconscious error in judging performance or work. Ratings that are either too favorable or too severe may result from a number of common errors, for example:

- the tendency to avoid the extremes of the scale and to rate at average;
- allowing an outstanding, or inferior, trait or aspect of performance to influence the rating of other factors (halo effect);
- judging according to a personal stereotype or strongly held (but not relevant) attitude;
- the tendency to prejudge individuals by an initial impression rather than on the basis of observed performance;
- the tendency to rate an individual more favorably if the person is similar to the rater in background, attitudes, or ethnic group;
- the tendency to rate someone lower than average when the assessment immediately follows an outstanding piece of evidence from someone else or to give a higher than average rating on an assessment immediately following evidence of a low level of learning by someone else (contrast effect).

5.5 It is essential to ensure that assessment is valid (i.e., that the assessor measures what is intended).

Ensure validity

Assessment will be valid if there are institutional guides as to what constitutes acceptable levels of learning, what learning is creditable to a particular credential or degree, what the established objectives of experiential learning programs are, and the specific learning goals for which students may have contracted.

It is important for institutions not only to describe learning that is creditable under various circumstances, but to provide illustrations whenever possible (i.e., examples of creditable learning as well as examples of learning that is not creditable and the reasons why). Similarly, assessment procedures that involve rating of products or performance should include clear examples of learning at different levels of competence.

5.51 Learning should be assessed by direct comparison with learning objectives or standards. (This principle is not meant to preclude recognition of unanticipated learning outcomes.)

5.52 Whenever appropriate, assessors should seek different forms of evidence of learning and use more than one type of assessment in order to reach a valid judgment.

5.6 An essential safeguard for quality assurance is provision for and an expectation of professional development for all personnel involved in the measurement of learning (Standard IX).

Train assessors, seek training as an assessor

5.61 Detailed written procedures, instructions, and background material should be sought out by and available to assessors concerning assessment procedures, particularly those routinely used.

5.62 Specialized assessment techniques, such as role-playing or simulation, should be used only by assessors who are sufficiently familiar with such methods and qualified to use them competently.

5.63 Standard conditions and arrangements for assessment should be maintained in accord with institutional guidelines. If the nature of the assessment problem suggests otherwise, deviations in procedures should be clarified and agreed to before implementation. When addressing the principle that assessment should fit the learning (Principles 5.1, 5.2), deviations from standardized practices may be required and become a common element of the process.

State results/ provide feedback

5.7 The results of individual assessment should be communicated clearly, with reference to the criteria on which it was based, and in a way that is likely to be understood and "heard" by the recipient (Standard III).

The outcome of the assessment should clearly identify what specific learning outcomes were involved, what levels of competence were reached, and what standards were employed. Appropriate assessment feedback enhances the quality of the assessment process itself by making it possible to compare assessments to determine how they were reached (Principles 5.4, 5.5).

Encourage and develop self- assessment skills

5.8 Self-assessment can be a significant aid to learning.

Self-assessment is a skill and an attitude that can be developed and encouraged through feedback. As with any other form of assessment, self-assessment should:

- express learning and not just a description of events or experiences (Standard I);

- relate performance or learning to the standards for the level of desired learning (Standard II) and learning objectives;
- convey what is or has been meaningful in the learning (Standard V); and
- contribute to the learning process as much as possible (Standard III).

5.81 Learner participation in both the design and administration of the assessment process is a means of enhancing personal development, particularly increasing self-managed learning skills.

Step 6. TRANSCRIPTION
Prepare a useful record of results.

Since experiential learning often emphasizes application of knowledge and the development of competence rather than a mastery of traditional theoretical and factual subject matter, usual course labels often do not adequately describe such learning. Learning from experience rarely comes neatly organized in course packages and may cover parts of two or more catalog courses. Given the particular objective of the learning and the pattern of learning already completed or planned, a precise convergence with catalog courses may not be possible. This is highly dependent on the crediting model that the institution or organization adopts (see Appendix A for definitions of block, course equivalence, and competence-based credit models).

However, the transcript credential is the only way many third parties will have evidence of the learning and how it contributes to a credential, degree, or other program objective. For these reasons, accurate descriptions and recordings of learning outcomes are important and integral parts of the assessment process. For the awarding institution, the maintenance of quality should already have been assured before reaching the transcribing process. For transfer institutions and other third parties, the transcript should contain the evidence needed to substantiate satisfaction of Standard I (credit for learning, not experience), Standard II (characteristics of the level of learning), Standard V (application to degree or other credential), and Standard VI (avoiding duplication). It is, however, not sufficient merely to indicate that credit was earned in an experiential learning program. Such a practice reflects and extends the error of confusing inputs (e.g., experiential learning activities) with learning outcomes (i.e., particular knowledge or skill competence).

Communicate with third parties	**6.1** Transcripts should communicate effectively with third parties, including other institutions and employers.

6.11 Institutions developing narrative transcripts should draw on user review panels to react to the proposed content and format. Appropriate reviewers include students, representatives of public and private employers, and graduate and professional admissions personnel.

6.12 In designing transcripts, it is desirable to attend carefully to *(a)* the need for clear description of the important, unique aspects of the individual student's learning and *(b)* the necessity to present succinct credentials that are likely to be given adequate attention by third parties.

Record learning appropriately	**6.2** Credit or other recognition of learning should be recorded on a transcript in a manner appropriate to the learning and to the function of the transcript as an accurate and comprehensive record of the individual's learning.

6.21 When learning is highly individualized, entering credit under arbitrary course labels is often misleading and may give an inaccurate impression of the learning outcomes gained. Some alternative is desirable (e.g., narrative descriptions, statement of outcomes using commonly accepted terms within the relevant disciplines).

6.22 Course labels or abbreviated descriptions of learning may be adequate when they refer to specific syllabi, detailed competence statements, or other information necessary for interpretation.

6.23 Regardless of the exact form of the credential, it is important that institutions strive to describe through the transcript what the individual knows or can do, not simply verify time served.

Describe content and level	**6.3** There are two essential elements of a good transcript. It must describe *(a)* the content of learning (i.e., what competence or knowledge was involved) and *(b)* the level of learning (i.e., what scope or depth was achieved). Both ends are served well if content and levels of competence are clearly differentiated in the statement of learning objectives.

6.31 When appropriate, transcripts should identify the auspices under which learning is acquired, especially when the conditions of learning and assessment differ.

6.32 Transcripts should include additional information to make clear the nature of the learning represented, such as dates when learning took place so that third parties might better judge whether learning is current; details such as location, supervision, or duration, which may bear upon quality of learning; an indication of how the learning was documented and assessed; and what standards were employed.

CHAPTER 5

Principles and Procedures for Assessing Unsponsored, Prior Experiential Learning

The prologue to this description of principles and procedures (see page 25) describes why the assessment of prior experiential learning[11] requires a different sequence of steps than those used in the assessment of learning from structured or sponsored events. Not only do the steps differ, but also the processes that accompany them. Learning from one's experience rarely comes in neat modules or packages the way course or other structured education-based learning does. Table 5.1 lists six steps for assessing prior experiential learning and relates them to the standards they serve. Given the idiosyncratic nature of unsponsored, prior experiential learning, there is less flexibility in following these steps than with sponsored experiential learning. Also, each step promises an educational function that can guide and reinforce the rigor of the assessment process.

TABLE 5.1	
The Assessment of Prior Experiential Learning	

STEPS	RELEVANT STANDARD(S)
1. IDENTIFICATION: Review experience to identify learning that is potentially creditable or appropriate for credentialing	*Standard I* Credit or its equivalent should be awarded only for learning and not for experience. *Standard III* Assessment should be treated as an integral part of learning, not separate from it, and should be based on an understanding of learning processes.
2. ARTICULATION: Relate proposed credit to academic, personal, and professional goals	*Standard II* Assessment should be based on standards and criteria for the level of acceptable learning that are both agreed upon and made public.

(continued)

---

[11] The term *prior experiential learning* excludes certain kinds of learning, both traditional and experiential, that have already been evaluated and transcribed. In this chapter we address that area of potentially college-creditable learning that has been acquired through work or other experience or that has been acquired through more traditional but not college-sponsored means, such as workshops and training courses in business, industry, or military settings.

TABLE 5.1

The Assessment of Prior Experiential Learning (CONTINUED)

2. ARTICULATION: *(continued)*	*Standard V* Credit or other credentialing should be appropriate to the context in which it is awarded and accepted.
3. DOCUMENTATION: Prepare evidence to support claim for credit	*Standard I* Credit or its equivalent should be awarded only for learning, and not for experience. *Standard II* Assessment should be based on standards and criteria for the level of acceptable learning that are both agreed upon and made public. *Standard III* Assessment should be treated as an integral part of learning, not apart from it, and should be based on an understanding of learning processes.
4. MEASUREMENT: Determine the degree and level of competence achieved	*Standard II* Assessment should be based on standards and criteria for the level of acceptable learning that are both agreed upon and made public. *Standard III* Assessment should be treated as an integral part of learning, not apart from it, and should be based on an understanding of learning processes. *Standard IV* The determination of competence levels and of credit awards must be made by appropriate subject matter and academic or credentialing experts.
5. EVALUATION: Determine the credit equivalency	*Standard II* Assessment should be based on standards and criteria for the level of acceptable learning that are both agreed upon and made public. *Standard IV* The determination of credit awards and competence levels must be made by appropriate subject matter and academic or credentialing experts. *Standard V* Credit or other credentialing should be appropriate to the context in which it is awarded and accepted.
6. TRANSCRIPTION: Prepare a useful record of results	*Standard VI* If awards are for credit, transcript entries should clearly describe what learning is being recognized and be monitored to avoid giving credit twice for the same learning.

These principles and procedures are also summarized in checklist form in Appendix C.

Step 1. IDENTIFICATION
Review experience to identify learning that is potentially creditable or appropriate for credentialing.

This is the entry point into the process for both a learner and whoever might be advising or coaching him/her through it. The nature of PLA is to ask—even expect—students to become agents of their own education in ways in which they probably lack experience. The mining of learning from experience requires patient exploration of possibilities—the perceived and desired relationship between the institution or organization, as well as the procedural elements of the assessment process. Indeed, attention to the nexus of these latter two elements is important throughout the process.

Helping students find the learning in the events of their lives when they may not have known previously how to think about those possibilities is a narrative process. Advisors who appreciate experience as a legitimate source of learning that derives from the multiple roles in adults' lives can help learners elicit possibilities for creditable learning. It is often difficult for the learners to identify these possibilities on their own. Engaging someone's memories and imagination in the course of identifying learning from contexts such as the workplace, volunteer activities, or family life can lead to new learning as well as reinforce what was already understood. Some element of new learning inevitably emerges from a re-examination of the known as well as experiences that lay tacit the first time around.

This is a critical stage in the assessment of prior experiential learning because of the obvious need to know as many of the possibilities of competencies or arenas of knowledge that may ultimately be assessed. It is also critical not to infer or arrive at judgments of creditability at this point. Those determinations will emerge in the later steps.

Many institutions encourage and often require the identification of learning derived from experience that may be creditable prior to or shortly after enrollment. Although difficult, this can be an important affirmation for adults who typically have some trepidation about venturing into formal education or training. However, there is no rule saying that prior learning must be identified and codified at the front end of a student's educational program. Recognizing and identifying experiential learning can occur at any point in one's life; thus, it can also occur at any point in one's educational or credentialing program.

The essence of this step lies in the characteristic of experiential learning (prior or recent) in that it lacks the advantage of preplanned learning objectives, learning activities, and assessment methods. Thus, the first important step in assessment is to discover and to describe learning that may have resulted from learning activities that did not include assessment as part of the process.

Develop strategies for describing learning experiences

1.1 Describing events and experiences can be a significant aid to recognizing and identifying learning. Advisors should develop strategies to help someone recall and record experiences that may be relevant or that hold significant learning potential (e.g., using a time line, resumé, work descriptions, or autobiography are techniques that represent a narrative strategy).

Differentiate between learning and experience

1.2 Over the course of the six steps, students will be required to differentiate between learning and experience (Standard I). The process for identifying potentially creditable learning should help someone learn and practice framing learning outcomes that she/he may claim in the course of describing various events and experiences.

Specify learning outcomes

1.3 A goal of the identification step should be to name the learning outcomes (i.e., what a person can do and/or knows) with enough specificity that these outcomes become the basis for the assessment steps that follow.

General terms like *communication*, *analysis*, or *management* can be useful in classifying learning outcomes but are not sufficient because they lack focus on specific learning outcomes. For example, to say that a person has learned to communicate may involve different skills at different levels of competence compared with someone else who claims knowledge/skill in communication. More specific descriptions of learning are necessary if a student and assessor(s) are to determine what might be creditable. More important, this process can go a long way toward recognizing when learning has, in fact, taken place.

1.31 The process of arriving at clarity and specificity in the identification of possible creditable learning can be informed by Standard II, the institutional or organizational standards for acceptable level and quality of learning. This process takes thought and patience, and should not be suppressed by premature judgments about whether this standard will be met.

Use assessment to promote and re-inforce learning

1.4 Identification of learning should proceed in a manner that reinforces what someone has learned, surfaces new insight or understanding, fosters heightened self-awareness, enhances self-confidence, and emphasizes the importance as well as the potential difficulties of students' assuming responsibility for their own learning (Standard III).

1.5 Specific mechanisms should be available that will not only help the student identify prior learning, but will also facilitate entry or re-entry into higher education or the credentialing body.

Language, procedures, assumptions, and other qualities that characterize a culture may be experienced as foreign and may inhibit students' seeking credit for prior learning. This is likely to be particularly true for those who have been absent from formal education for some time and may be unsure of themselves as learners as well as unsure about how to proceed in an unfamiliar system.

The process of developing evidence of prior learning can be difficult. With proper support, however, it frequently proves to be a valuable learning experience in itself. Consequently, institutions or organizations should seriously consider providing some formal mechanism for assisting people—possibilities include counseling, mentoring, workshops, educational planning courses, and self-instructional materials.

1.51 Students should be provided with explanatory materials concerning assessment of prior learning, including examples of portfolio materials.

1.52 Institutions or programs should seriously consider implementing a formal course to orient learners to the assessment of experience-based learning (i.e., a sponsored experiential learning event to help the assessment of unsponsored experiential learning). The identification step is more than the beginning of the assessment process; it is also an opportunity for students to learn about how they learn and perhaps even advance their capacities for learning in the future (i.e., learning how to learn).

A credit-bearing course in an educational context has many other advantages. It signals serious intent and acknowledges that helping learners acquire expertise in educational planning and assessment is valued in the institution. Such a course magnifies the educational value of assessment. It also provides a vehicle for monitoring a learner's progress and providing assistance as needed. Furthermore, a formal course recognizes the faculty time devoted to assessment as a legitimate instructional cost.

Step 2. ARTICULATION
Relate proposed credit to academic, personal, and professional goals.

In Step 2, the learner, along with a representative of the institution or organization (e.g., faculty advisor), must relate the claimed and potentially creditable learning to the requirements of the relevant academic or credentialing program (Standard V). Ideally, this is also a triangulation process that relates the outcomes of the identification step to the learner's personal and career goals. Thus, there are at least two components to the articulation step: an expression of the personal and an institutional context for the learning outcomes to be assessed. Consequently, the outcomes of the articulation step are several: *(a)* further definition of the learning outcomes that may be creditable; *(b)* affirmation of the value of learning gained through experience; *(c)* separation of the institutionally and personally meaningful learning outcomes from those that may only be meaningful to the individual or other contexts; and *(d)* the emergence of the outline of a plan for the remaining steps of the assessment process. Minimally, however, the validity of an arena of learning from experience for credit purposes depends upon a demonstrated relationship to a defined degree (or program) or credentialing objective.

Because the articulation step follows the identification step, the standards for the level of acceptable learning merge into the process as another criterion for sorting likely from unlikely creditable learning. As is the case for sponsored learning, the fact that learning is determined to meet a particular standard, such as college level, is not ordinarily a sufficient basis for granting college credit. The insertion of Standard II at this point differs from the assessment process for sponsored learning. In the latter (sponsored learning), an immediate threshold is evident. In prior experiential learning, the learner—and whoever is helping her/him—uses the process to arrive at how an area of learning articulates with the program or personal goals. The principles and procedures discussed in this section support quality assurance with respect to Standard V (learning must be appropriate to academic context).

| Determine what is creditable | **2.1** Each institution or organization should have a published rationale for crediting particular types of learning in each of its programs or offerings. As program requirements respond to changes in society or professions and seek to serve the unique needs of individual learners, institutions should have published processes for making exceptions and extending or changing the rationale for determining what is creditable. |

| Align the articulation with the criteria for an acceptable level of learning outcomes | **2.2** Each institution or organization should make public its criteria for determining the levels of learning (Standard II).

2.21 At the articulation step, issues or questions may need to be addressed in the ensuing steps as they may relate to both Standard II and relevant policies—for example, currency of learning (Principle 2.4) and limits to the amount of credit that may be earned in a PLA process.

2.3 Institutions should require learners seeking credit to specify satisfactorily how prior experiential learning contrib- |

| Relate proposed creditable learning to program objectives |

utes to the individual's degree, other program objectives, or the credential being sought.

2.31 Institutions or organizations should support a process to help learners realize and specify learning goals and their relationship to both prior learning and program objectives. A student may need the assistance of an advisor or coach to identify his/her learning goals.

In identifying and articulating learning that is related to educational goals, the student should look both backward and forward—backward to integrate past learning and to identify important gaps, and forward to plan continued learning that builds effectively on the foundation of the prior learning assessment.

2.32 Learning goals and related experiential learning should be "mined" to enhance self-awareness and personal development as well as the extent and level of knowledge or competencies that may be creditable.

| Consider the recency of learning |

2.4 There should be a stated policy with respect to the recency or currency of learning outcomes if there is anticipation that credit may be awarded. This policy should avoid inconsistencies with existing practices of the institution or organization in transcript evaluation of students transferring credits from other programs.

It is difficult to determine exactly when this principle should be introduced into the process. It is advisable to get a sense of the currency early in case there may be a question of limits. One of two decisions may be made: Drop this specific area of learning from consideration because of the policy or anticipate that additional learning may be required before bringing the outcomes to the step of documentation and measurement. However, caution should be taken in raising questions of currency too early in the process in order to avoid communicating an unintended deterrent to seeking credit for prior learning.

Step 3. DOCUMENTATION
Prepare evidence to support claim for credit.

Documentation of experiential learning can come in many forms. The documentation must fit or support the stated learning objectives or outcomes. The wider the range of acceptable forms that evidence may take, the more possibilities there are for fitting one or more forms of documentation to the learning. Different types of documentation act as media for the expression of various manifestations of learning. And the process of creating the evidence of learning can serve several different functions for the student: for example, *(a)* to learn ways of organizing what one knows or can do for presentation to others or for one's self, even if it serves no administrative purpose; *(b)* to accumulate descriptive information over time that may become useful to both a student and an advisor for assessment purposes; *(c)* to prepare for consulting with third-party expertise; and *(d)* to serve as a record for both the student and the institution/organization.

Documentation may include direct, or primary, evidence of learning, such as work samples or other products of learning. It may also include secondary evidence of learning in the form of certificates, letters of testimony from appropriate and qualified witnesses to someone's learning, and achievement awards. Further, it may include demonstrations, the outcomes of simulations or performances. The determining factors for deciding what appropriate documentation can and/or should look like are the convergence of flexibility, imagination, qualifications of assessors, and the nature of the learning to be evidenced. Presentation of adequate evidence of learning is a vital step in the assessment process and a prerequisite for quality assurance in achieving Standards I and II in ways that honor Standard III.

Base assessment on evidence

3.1 Assessment of learning from experience should be based on learning for which there is evidence. This is an implication of Standard I, the assurance that credit or credentialing should be based on learning, not experience. Any exceptions that recognize experience as a proxy for learning should be clearly justified and spelled out by policy.

3.11 Institutions should formulate policies regarding documentation and what function(s) documentation is intended to serve.

Reference what is creditable

3.2 As stated in Principle 2.1, each institution or organization should have a published rationale for crediting particular types of learning in each of its programs or offerings. As program requirements respond to changes in society or professions and seek to serve unique needs of individual learners, institutions should make public their processes for making exceptions as well as for extending or changing the rationale for determining what is creditable. (See Standard II.)

Evaluators should reference Standard II throughout the assessment process. It is introduced here, at the point of documentation, to highlight that the first two steps are borne of an interest in bringing out the possibilities for creditable learning without prematurely judging its merits relative to Standard II. The student should have the opportunity to develop the evidence of learning before it is measured and evaluated.

Develop
perspectives and
policies on primary
and secondary
forms of evidence
and documentation

3.3 The relative values of primary and secondary forms of evidence of prior or experiential learning should be a part of the formulation of an institution's or organization's guidelines for good practice.

3.31 There should be clear specifications as to what types of documentation are appropriate for what types of learning.

3.32 Students should be provided with descriptions and examples of different types of documentation, the functions they serve, and how they should be solicited and presented. Types of documentation might include the following: *(a)* verification of accomplishment (e.g., a prize or musical program); *(b)* testimony regarding competence (e.g., evaluative letters or job performance reports); *(c)* learning products (e.g., learning logs, essays, work samples, or art objects); *(d)* certification (e.g., licenses or rank attained); *(e)* other direct evidence (e.g., publications or test scores); and *(f)* descriptions (e.g., syllabi, membership requirements, or job descriptions).

3.33 Guidelines for documentation should make clear in what ways documentation could be used in assessment.

3.34 Documentation of a student's participation in a learning activity as part of her/his experiential learning should not, in itself, constitute adequate evidence of learning.

3.4 Assessors should take all reasonable and necessary steps to ensure that evidence of learning is accurate and that the student is, in fact, responsible for work presented. There should be public guidelines as to what constitutes authentic documentation.

3.41 Authentication procedures for evidence transmitted electronically or through Internet-based interactions are still evolving. Procedures for authentication should represent a combination of appropriate technology and decisions regarding the message regarding trust that an institution or organization wants to communicate through its language, policies, and procedures.

3.42 When documenting learning by testimony, procedures for obtaining letters to document learning should emphasize attention to the nature of the learning and the dependability of the source of evidence.

Individuals writing such letters should know the student, be free of any conflict of interests, and have firsthand knowledge of the experiential learning cited. A documentation letter should state the nature of the author's relationship with the student and the author's credentials as an expert judge (Standard IV). If appropriate, the letter should be written on official stationery.

3.43 Either the student or the assessor—or both—should make clear to those providing documentation that they are to provide evidence of the level and depth of learning, not a recommendation of credit, grading, or credentialing.

Judge quality, not quantity

3.5 Evaluators should take care to ensure that the quantity and the attractiveness of the presentation of evidence do not influence the award or credit or its equivalent. Credit awards must be based on learning, not experience (Standard I) and on accurate measurement of the quality and depth of learning at the desired level (Standard II).

Documentation contributes to learning

3.6 The process of creating or gathering evidence of learning is as much a part of the learning process as the experiences and reflection upon them are. Documenting learning is a strategy as well as a part of the reflective process and should be treated as such (Standard III); guidelines, examples, and feedback on documentation can be manifestations of this standard.

Step 4. MEASUREMENT
Determine the degree and level of learning/competence achieved.

Measuring learning and determining credit constitute the heart of the assessment process. This step in assessment involves determining the extent and character of the knowledge or skill acquired. The principles and procedures that are followed in this part of the process will support the achievement of several of the ten standards. Perhaps most important, these principles and procedures are clearly related to Standard IV (ensuring that competency judgments are made by qualified experts) as well as Standard II (assessment should be based on standards and criteria for the level of acceptable learning that are agreed upon and made public) and Standard III (assessment should be treated as an integral part of learning, not separate from it, and should be based on an understanding of learning processes).

For assessors, the assessment process is an opportunity to promote learning through feedback on the learner's insights, strengths, gaps in knowledge or skill, and areas for further development as well as through general, informative commentary. This aspect of assessment—and all the principles derived from the standards—brings the measurement step into a close relationship with one particular standard, Standard IX (the role of adequate training of assessors).

Finally, accuracy of judgment is essential since inconsistency among judges is unfair to students and may discredit the assessment process.

Quality assurance depends on both the reliability (Principle 4.5) and validity (Principle 4.6) of the measurement process.

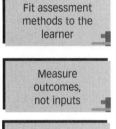

Fit assessment method to the learning

Fit assessment methods to the learner

Measure outcomes, not inputs

Utilize assessment as learning

4.1 Assessment of experiential learning should employ measurement methods that fit the character of the learning and the outcomes intended to be measured. Intentions to measure reconstructive learning outcomes should not be measured by strategies or techniques that elicit data regarding reproductive learning and vice versa.

Much experiential learning is characterized by different learning outcomes for different individuals and, thus, may require differing assessment strategies from person to person to person. An assessment strategy may include standardized testing, but it should not be the only method of assessment.

4.2 In measuring an individual's learning, assessors should use techniques that are appropriate to the background and characteristics of the learner. This principle calls for advisors to take into account differences among people, including limitations and differences associated with disabilities.

4.3 Assessment of experiential learning should place emphasis upon criterion-referenced assessment so that individuals are evaluated in terms of expected learning outcomes, not on time on task or activity (Standard I).

4.4 The measurement of learning can be a useful learning experience in itself and construed as part of the overall learning event (Standard III).

4.41 The best assessment strategies create opportunities for additional learning as well as measure what has already been learned (Standard III). Because the measurement of learning gained from experience is often a retrospective process, care should be taken not to treat it as an audit. This can be particularly avoided by including learners in the assessment processes and the function they serve. An appreciation of the purpose of assessment can help reinforce an individual's responsibility for his/her own learning and a sense of mutual accountability with the assessor.

Formative assessment and measurement of experiential learning can be a very powerful aid to the process. This may be particularly true when self-assessment and assessing the quality of self-assessment are included as part of the formative assessment. Improved self-awareness and better understanding of the techniques of assessment applied to one's self (i.e., self-assessment) are in themselves learning outcomes of assessment. Thus, the greater extent to which assessment is experienced as a mix of feedback, instruction, evaluation, and measurement of learning, the greater the likelihood that self-managed learning can be developed. Both the formative and summative stages of evaluative measurement offer opportunities to develop this outcome.

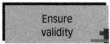

4.5 Institutions should strive for assessment that is as reliable (i.e., consistent) as possible in order to ensure fairness to students.

4.51 When possible, the assessment of more than one sample of evidence of learning can improve consistency in assessment judgments.

4.52 Unless there is evidence that indicated one assessor is sufficient, or financial constraints are prohibitive, more than one assessor should be used. Different assessors can vary considerably in their judgments, especially if they have had limited experience with assessment or if assessment guidelines are not clear.

4.53 Assessors should strive to avoid bias, discrimination, or unconscious error in judging performance or work. Ratings that are either too favorable or too severe may result from a number of common errors, for example:

- the tendency to avoid the extremes of the scale and to rate at average;
- allowing an outstanding, or inferior, trait or aspect of performance to influence the rating of other factors (halo effect);
- judging according to a personal stereotype or strongly held (but not relevant) attitude;
- the tendency to prejudge individuals by an initial impression rather than on the basis of observed performance;
- the tendency to rate an individual more favorably if the person is similar to the rater in background, attitudes, or ethnic group;
- the tendency to rate someone lower than average when the assessment immediately follows an outstanding piece of evidence from someone else or to give a higher than average rating on an assessment immediately following evidence of a low level of learning by someone else (contrast effect).

4.6 It is essential to ensure that assessment is valid (i.e., that the assessor measures what is intended to be measured).

Assessment will be valid if there are institutional guides as to what constitutes acceptable levels of learning, what learning is creditable to a particular credential or degree, what the established objectives of experiential learning programs are, and the specific learning goals for which students may have contracted.

It is important for institutions not only to describe learning that is creditable under various circumstances, but to provide illustrations, when possible (i.e., examples of creditable learning as well as examples of learning that are not creditable and the reasons why). Similarly, assessment procedures that involve rating products or performance should clearly describe learning at different levels of competence as well as provide examples of each.

4.61 Learning should be assessed by direct comparison with learning objectives or criterion standards. (This principle is not meant to preclude recognition of unanticipated learning outcomes.)

4.62 Whenever appropriate, assessors should seek different forms of evidence of learning and use more than one type of assessment in order to reach a valid judgment.

Train assessors, seek training as an assessor

4.7 An essential safeguard for quality assurance is a provision for and an expectation of professional development for all personnel involved in the measurement of learning (Standard IX).

4.71 Detailed written procedures, instructions, and background material should be sought out by and made available to assessors concerning assessment procedures, particularly those routinely used.

4.72 Specialized assessment techniques, such as role-playing or simulation should be used only by assessors who are sufficiently familiar with such methods and qualified to use them competently.

4.73 Standard conditions and arrangements for assessment should be maintained in accord with institutional guidelines. If the nature of the assessment problem suggests otherwise, deviations in procedures should be clarified and agreed to beforehand. When adhering to the principle that assessment should fit the learning (Principles 5.1, 5.2), this may become a common element of the process.

State results/ provide feedback

4.8 The results of individual assessment should be communicated clearly, with reference to the criteria on which it was based, and in a way that is likely to be understood and "heard" by the recipient (Standard III).

The outcome of the assessment should be as explicit as possible in identifying what specific learning outcomes were involved, what levels of competence were reached, and what standards were employed. Assessment feedback communicated with these characteristics facilitates quality of the assessment process itself by making it possible to compare assessments to determine how they were reached (Principles 5.4, 5.5).

4.9 Self-assessment can be a significant aid to learning.

Encourage and develop self-assessment skills ◾

Self-assessment is a skill and an attitude that can be developed and encouraged through feedback. As with any other form of assessment, self-assessment should:

- express learning and not just describe events or experiences (Standard I);
- relate performance or learning to the standards for the level of desired learning (Standard II) and learning objectives;
- convey what is or has been meaningful in the learning (Standard V); and
- contribute to the learning process as much as possible (Standard III).

4.91 Learner participation in both the design and administration of the assessment process is a means of enhancing personal development, particularly increasing self-managed learning skills. (See also 4.3.)

Step 5. EVALUATION
Determine the credit equivalency.

Unlike the assessment of sponsored learning, PLA requires that measurement (How much has been learned, and at what level of competence?—See Step 4) must be completed before evaluation (Does the learning meet acceptable standards and, if so, how much credit should be awarded?). Since this is the crucial and final step before any credit should be awarded for prior learning, it is not surprising that it is directly related to nearly all of the standards.

In determining the amount of credit, assessors or other personnel of the assessment program should look beyond the confirmation (or denial) of the learning claimed in the first steps. The assessment process may have identified creditable learning, but it may also have identified that some or all of the claimed learning may be creditable only after additional learning (e.g., through course work or independent study). The evaluation step is also an opportunity to review the learner's academic, personal, and career goals, taking advantage of new insights resulting from the results of the assessment.

Decide who categorizes and defines competencies ◾

5.1 Institutional policy concerning the standard-setting authority should be clear. Standards may be defined on the basis of institutional program objectives, the objectives of students, or the requirements of third parties (occupational or educational). When the context fits, it is desirable to take all three into account.

5.2 Criteria have to be established on which to evaluate the level of learning (Standard II) and the amount of credit or the credential that should be awarded.

5.21 An individual's learning should be assessed in relation to criteria that set out indicators by which to measure the level of learning/competence.

In defining standards, levels of competence should be clearly stated and illustrated by examples. When several levels of competence are defined, different individuals in different programs or institutions might quite rightly receive credit or recognition for different levels of competence depending upon the nature of the program.

5.22 The process should employ expertise both in subject matter content and in evaluation (Standard IX).

5.23 All criteria for awarding credit should be rigorous and reasonable in relation to the goals and character of the institution and the nature of its students.

5.3 The model and basis for awarding credit should be established.

5.31 There are several models and approaches for connecting learning outcomes with credit or credit equivalencies. For example, credit hour equivalencies can be established for particular accomplishments; learning outcomes can be matched with those of existing courses; competencies may be recognized with or without regard to credit hours (i.e., the system is entirely competence-based); or blocks of credit that don't fit existing course structures may be judged to represent breadth and depth of learning derived from Standard II criteria. The choice of credit model should be rationalized and recorded by the institution or organization.

Academic hours may be estimated for purposes of predicting what learning activities may be necessary to meet some outcome expectations but should not be relied on for direct translation of experience into learning for credit or its equivalent. Formal guidelines are especially desirable to ensure equity in awards.

5.32 The extent of possible credit or credentialing someone who may be awarded should be made clear at the beginning of the process and then justified at this evaluation step, following the documentation and measurement of learning.

5.33 The basis for translating outcomes into credit hours or credential thresholds should be specified. Time spent in an activity should not be a primary consideration for determining credit or credential equivalency.

5.34 Consideration should be given to a system of credit or credentialing that accommodates the awarding of varying amounts of credit or levels of credentialing based on the assessment of the experiential learning.

5.4 Standards for crediting or recognizing experiential learning should be the same as, or comparable to, standards for crediting or recognizing learning by other means.

5.41 The basis for translating outcomes into credit hours or credential thresholds should be specified. Time spent in an activity should not be a primary consideration for determining credit or credential equivalency (see Principle 5.31).

5.5 Assessment of experiential learning should place emphasis upon criterion-referenced assessment so that individuals are evaluated in terms of learning outcomes, not on time-on-task or activity (Standard I).

5.6 Evaluation (relationship of learning to credit/credentialing and grades) and measurement (determination of depth and level of learning) should be formative as well as summative (Standard III).

5.61 Establish guidelines for the quality and characteristics of good feedback.

5.62 A review of prior learning should precede each new learning activity and relate it to the learner's objective.

5.63 Summative feedback should be provided as soon as possible after the completion of the evaluation and measurement of the learning. It should include explanation of credit or credential awards and implications for program or degree requirements. The summative evaluation should also serve as the initial step in planning future learning (Principle 5.61).

5.63 In providing feedback concerning evaluation and credits awarded (or not awarded), it is important to discuss implications for degree or credential requirements.

5.64 Appropriate mechanisms should be developed to assist a student in integrating the results of PLA and evaluation into her/his educational program. PLA should be recognized as the foundation for planning sponsored learning and not solely as a means of acquiring credit.

5.65 Extend advising on the outcomes of an assessment to include plans for future learning.

5.7 Institutions or organizations should consider multiple or alternative uses for evaluated learning, such as granting advanced standing or waiving some requirements.

5.71 Options for awarding credit or credentialing may be associated with less-than-complete demonstrations of learning from experience at the level for which credit or credentialing is being requested when the learning constitutes adequate preparation to undertake studies for which some prerequisites are normally expected.

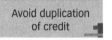
Provide for review and appeal

5.8 There should be a provision, of which students are advised, whereby credit awards can be appealed if there appears to be due cause.

5.81 The regular review of individual credit awards should be a part of an established, more comprehensive process of periodic review of the entire prior-learning credit process (Standard X).

Avoid duplication of credit

5.9 In recommending credit awards, evaluators should take necessary steps to guard against duplication of credit (Standard VI).

Step 6. TRANSCRIPTION
Prepare a useful record of results.

Since experiential learning often emphasizes application of knowledge and the development of competence rather than a mastery of traditional theoretical and factual subject matter, usual course labels often do not adequately describe such learning. Learning from experience rarely comes neatly organized in course packages and may cover parts of two or more catalog courses. Given the particular objective of the learning and the pattern of learning already completed or planned, a precise convergence with catalog courses may not be possible. This is highly dependent on the crediting model that the institution or organization adopts (see Appendix A for definitions of block, course equivalence, and competence-based credit models).

However, the transcript credential is the only way many third parties will have evidence of the learning and how it contributes to a credential, degree, or other program objective. For these reasons, accurate descriptions and recordings of learning outcomes are an important and integral part of the assessment process. For the awarding institution, the maintenance of quality should already have been assured before reaching the transcribing process. For transfer institutions and other third parties, the transcript should contain the evidence needed to substantiate satisfaction of Standard I (credit for learning, not experience), Standard II (characteristics of the level of learning), Standard V (application to degree or other credential), and Standard VI (avoiding duplication). It is, however, not sufficient merely to indicate that credit was earned in an experiential learning program. Such a practice reflects and extends the error of confusing inputs (e.g., experiential learning activities) with learning outcomes (i.e., particular knowledge or skill competence).

Step 6, transcribing the results of the assessment process to this point, is usually an administrative function. However, in the case of prior learning outcomes it is particularly important for the assessor to provide sufficient information about the measurement and evaluation judgments to help the transcription process to meet the requirements of Standard VI (avoid duplication). Finally, transcription can be a way to highlight institutional or organizational support for the assessment of learning gained through experience(s) and to help legitimize it.

Communicate with third parties

6.1 Transcripts should communicate effectively with third parties (e.g., employers, admission officers, professional associations) considering decisions based on the assessed experiential learning, such as application for work or further study.

6.11 In designing transcripts or transcript entries, it is desirable to balance carefully *(a)* the need for clear description of the important, and often unique, aspects of the individual student's learning, and *(b)* the necessity to present succinct credentials that are likely to be given adequate attention by third parties.

6.12 Credit or other recognition of experiential learning should be recorded in a manner appropriate to the learning and to the function of the transcript as an accurate and comprehensive record of the individual's learning.

6.13 Institutions developing narrative transcripts should appoint user review panels to provide feedback on the proposed content and format. Appropriate reviewers include students, representatives of public and private employers, and graduate and professional admissions personnel.

Set policies regarding the content of transcripts or transcript entries

6.2 There are two essential elements of a good transcript: *(a)* the content of learning (i.e., what competence or knowledge was involved) and *(b)* the level of learning (i.e., what scope or depth was achieved).

6.21 Beyond these basics, the options for additional information include:

- the context or auspices under which learning is acquired;
- dates when learning was assessed (so that third parties might better judge whether learning is still current);
- an explanation of how the learning was documented and assessed; and
- what standards were employed in the assessment of learning (Standard II).

6.3 When learning is highly individualized, entering credit under arbitrary course labels is often misleading and may give inaccurate impressions about the nature of the learning. Some alternative is desirable, such as the use of narrative descriptions or statements of outcomes.

6.31 Course labels or abbreviated descriptions of learning may be adequate for transcripts when they refer to specific syllabi or detailed competence statements. In such cases, descriptive information necessary for interpretation should be part of the transcript or should be readily available.[12]

6.32 Regardless of the exact form of the credential, it is important that institutions strive to describe through the transcript what the student knows or can do, not simply to verify time served.

---

[12] When the credits that are awarded are expressed in terms of stated learning outcomes, this procedure (Principle 6.31) should not be necessary. Ideally, all transcripts would describe the level and content of skills and knowledge acquired (i.e., the learning outcomes). The sources of the learning would be irrelevant. Realistically, however, many consumers of transcripts still base important decisions on their perceptions of the source of learning, rather than on its level and content. Until this practice disappears, it is unfair to learners not to specify the sources of learning on the transcript.

CHAPTER

6

Administrative Measures to Assure Quality

It is not enough to achieve a level of quality—the level must also be maintained. *Quality assurance* is the collective term for institutional or organizational activities, policies, and procedures that guarantee the following: a positive impact on learning at the level(s) established internally and externally, continued achievement of the institution's goals, and adherence to the spirit as well as substance of the standards and principles of learning assessment.

It is not possible to draw a sharp line between the academic standards addressed in relation to assessment steps (chapters four and five) and the administrative standards that are the focus of this chapter. Many of the administrative principles and procedures also appear in the discussion of academic principles and procedures for sponsored and prior experiential learning assessment.

There are, however, additional administrative threads in the fabric of quality assurance. These relate particularly to Standards VII, VIII, IX, and X (publication of policies, cost of assessment, development of assessors, and program evaluation). Standard VI (avoiding duplication) is covered in the preceding chapters in relation to transcription of credited learning (Principle 6 in both sponsored learning and prior learning).

Of course, administrative safeguards pertaining to each standard should be included in each institution's administrative policies and procedures. The principles and procedures that follow are not offered as sequential steps extending the six assessment steps in each of the sections on academic principles and procedures. They are, however, numbered corresponding to Standards VII, VIII, IX, and X.

Principles and procedures related to Standard VII:
"Policies, procedures, and criteria applied to assessment, including provision for appeal, should be fully disclosed and prominently available for all parties involved in the assessment process."

Transparent, readily accessible information on a program, including its assessment process, demonstrates respect for everyone associated with the program. Everything from a program's underlying philosophy to its assessment procedures should be made available to administrators, students, faculty, assessors, and advisors. This is true for the most well-established programs as well as those that depart significantly from common practices. (A model for a comprehensive policy is included in Appendix D.)

In order to be effective, a policy should be published in a place where it is accessible to each audience and should contain procedures for its distribution. This may entail inclusion in a wide range of organizational or campus documents, including the official catalog, staff and faculty manuals, program booklets, guidelines, flyers, and other types of advertising.

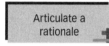

Articulate a rationale

7.1 The institution or organization should articulate a clear rationale for fostering, assessing, and crediting or credentialing learning gained from experience, especially as it reflects the nature of the institution's/organization's mission or purposes.

7.11 The rationale or statement of purpose should be written at a level that helps or informs decision making, particularly when there are significant options from which to choose a direction.

Clarify review processes

7.2 The process of formal review, approval, and revision of the rationale, policies, and procedures should be articulated. It also should be subject to and related to the processes for regular review of the academic procedures of the institution or organization in order to ensure the legitimacy of the assessment activities.

7.21 Each level of review or approval of policies or procedures should contribute to the quality of these components.

Provide clear policies and practices based on an integrated curriculum

7.3 To integrate experiential learning into a curriculum, requirements for degrees or credentials should be stated as reasonably specific learning outcomes in such forms as types of knowledge, competencies, or disposition rather than in general terms of some specific number of courses or units.

7.31 Faculty or other qualified personnel should examine systematically what types of experiential learning can or may contribute most effectively to attainment of credential or degree requirements.

7.32 It is important to clarify how assessment and experiential learning programs operate in relation to other components of the institution and to ensure that policies and procedures are well integrated with those of other departments and functions.

7.33 It is useful to develop an operational model that describes how an experiential learning program operates within the institution.

Clarify roles and responsibilities

7.4 Roles and responsibilities of all persons involved with the assessment—assessors, students, administrators, faculty, and advisors—should be clearly described in a comprehensive policies and procedures guide provided to all involved.

Provide handbook with information on policies, procedures, roles, and responsibilities

7.5 Whatever the size of the experiential learning program may be, comprehensive written guidelines should be created and kept current. Written guidelines result in a level of public scrutiny that ensures accountability. They also ensure that policies are interpreted and applied consistently, and increase efficiency when bringing in new faculty and students.

7.51 Desirable components of such a handbook include program rationale, assessment procedures, standards, crediting policies, administrative procedures, and examples of documents and relevant forms.

7.52 All students participating in either a sponsored program of experiential learning or an assessment of unsponsored experiential learning should receive the same handbook as other program personnel.

In addition, there should be appropriate information for students considering participating in any experiential program or assessment of prior learning. This material should contain sufficient information to permit students to make an informed judgment as to whether participation is likely to prove useful, cost-effective, and worth the student's time. For example, a flow diagram showing how someone proceeds through steps and decision points may be especially helpful in describing the process.

7.53 Program administrators must make sure that there is "truth in advertising" and that students are not misled about costs, the time and effort required, or the amount of credit that they will earn. Under no circumstances should there be any implied promises that any credit will be awarded (Standard VIII).

Protect individual privacy

7.6 There should be established procedures regarding the handling and filing of student portfolios and other materials related to assessment in order to protect the privacy of students and others. Statutes and regulations at the local or national levels may govern these policies and procedures and, thus, should be made available to all involved.

Determine perspectives and policies regarding individual differences

7.7 Policies regarding the responsiveness of an assessment program to individual differences should be formulated. Such policies should consider legal as well as organizational precedents regarding both the definition of norms and the range of accommodation given to individuals who do not fit those norms.

Principles and procedures related to Standard VIII:
"Fees charged for assessment should be based on the services performed in the process and not determined by the amount of credit awarded."

As stated in chapter 3, the essential premise of this standard is that the cost of instruction in course-based programs is the same whether a student passes the course and is awarded credit or fails and receives no credit. This relationship between fees and credit must be replicated in programs that assess experiential learning in order to preserve quality.

Financing is a critical aspect of assessing experiential learning with respect to both cost effectiveness and pricing. Consequently, quality assurance necessitates a complete financial analysis of the costs of the program and revenue required to maintain it. The financial model will determine the overall health of the assessment program.

The highly individual character of experiential learning often necessitates individualized assessment. Fees should be structured on the basis of assessment effort, not on credit awarded. Pricing assessment, and accounting for its cost, raises a host of administrative questions that are vital to a program's operation and success, and the choice of assessment methods that are adopted and supported must take cost into account.

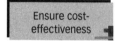
Charge fees for assessment, not for credit

8.1 Care should be taken to ensure that there is never an appearance of buying credit.

8.11 It should be made clear to all parties what services will be provided for an assessment fee (e.g., review of documentation, feedback, number of times documentation may be submitted for review following revision, transcribing).

8.12 Fees may vary by the amount of credit sought or attempted to be awarded, based on the rationale that time and effort by assessors is likely to be relative to the complexity of the evidence of learning.

8.13 Fees should be charged regardless of the assessment outcome.

Ensure cost-effectiveness

8.2 Institutions or organizations should ensure through careful analysis of direct and indirect costs that procedures for assessing experiential learning are cost-effective with respect to the interests of students, the institution, and broader social considerations.

8.21 Care should be taken to allocate costs of assessment and its financing in ways that are equitable to students as consumers and to assessors and administration as providers.

| Recognize assessment as a contribution to learning | **8.3** Analysis of the cost of assessment should take into account its contribution to the learning function of the institution or organization in ways parallel or equivalent to other instructional functions. |

A sound assessment procedure, for example, should not be sacrificed simply because it appears to be more expensive than traditional assessment methods. If assessment of experiential learning is designed to have direct educational benefit, it might well be considered an instructional cost.

8.31 Remuneration to assessors of prior experiential learning should be based upon effort and expertise, not the number of credit hours awarded.

| Monitor cost-effectiveness and efficiency | **8.4** Institutions should constantly work to improve the validity, reliability, and efficiency of assessment procedures so as to improve cost-effectiveness without reducing the quality of assessment or its usefulness to students. |

8.41 Special assessment procedures should be worth what they cost the student; prices should reflect the real cost of assessment as well as the real benefit of the assessment process itself.

Principles and procedures related to Standard IX:
"All personnel involved in the assessment of learning should pursue and receive adequate training and continuing professional development for the functions they perform."

This is perhaps the cornerstone of quality assurance. There is a reciprocal responsibility for both assessors and the institutions/organizations/agencies that provide learning assessment. From the institutional or organizational perspective, before providing adequate training for assessors, the institution must *(a)* set desired outcomes of professional development based on the standards and principles of assessment that it adopts; *(b)* decide who is involved with the process; *(c)* define roles and specify responsibilities for all of the parties; and *(d)* decide what constitutes accountability for performance. From the perspective of the personnel (e.g., staff, faculty/assessors, administrators), pursuit of a high-level work performance depends on initial training, continued workplace learning, and support in terms of both time and appropriate resources from the organization.

It is wise to organize the learning needs of the organization around both the functions associated with each step in the assessment of sponsored and unsponsored learning and the skills required to act in accordance with the standards and principles. In practice, a good deal of cooperation and collaboration among people with various functions are required to carry out a high-quality assessment program. This aspect of quality assurance needs to be recognized in training and professional development efforts as well. Functions such as *(a)* mentoring or helping the student define and pursue learning and assessment objectives; *(b)* making judgments about the character and level of learning; and *(c)* determining the value of learning in credits or other academic currency may or may not be carried out by the same person. Awareness of all the roles and responsibilities can go a long way toward ensuring a quality experience for the student.

Policies for training and professional development should include the students or professionals seeking assessment of their learning. In addition to informing them of what they need to know to participate directly in the assessment of their learning, institutions/organizations should be prepared to help them understand as much as they wish to know about assessment itself.

Identify who can and should participate in the assessment process and determine their respective roles

9.1 Institutions and organizations need to determine who is appropriate to contribute to the assessment process and what the qualifications are for participation.

9.11 The determination of who should participate should be based on a clear rationale.

Some institutions or programs only permit faculty to serve as assessors in the evaluation or measurement of learning; others seek community expertise outside of the institution or organization. Each approach has justification and carries implications for quality assurance.

Assessors can be subject matter experts, assessment experts, or faculty concerned with generic competencies not associated with a particular discipline. They may or may not include individuals outside the institution. The role of outside experts, however, is usually confined to judging knowledge and competence levels attained. Faculty members of the institution awarding the credit must make the determination of credit awards. Policies regarding choice of assessors should reflect the nature of the program and the types of learning involved.

9.12 If the role of expert or assessment resource person is open to individuals outside of the faculty, various evidence should be provided that qualify that person as an expert (e.g., publications or awards, recommendations of other experts, professional position, etc.).

Determine the number of assessors who should evaluate an individual's learning

Specify responsibilities of assessors and associated personnel

Create a culture of quality assurance through continued learning

9.2 The institution or organization should determine how many assessors should participate in the evaluation of an individual's learning. Reliability and cost are considerations that should be taken into account.

9.3 The responsibilities of assessors, experts, and other assessment resource persons should be clearly specified.

9.31 Training and professional development should be designed to help each person meet the responsibilities of his/her role.

9.32 A broad understanding of assessment as well as the technical aspects of assessment methods should be expected both of the institution or organization and of personnel.

9.33 Assessors should be competent not only in the subject matter of their assessment but also in the principles and limitations of the assessment technique employed.

9.4 The responsible administrator(s) and assessment personnel in the institution should make every effort to create an expectation of quality assurance through learning.

9.41 All individuals participating in an aspect of assessment should receive initial training appropriate to those responsibilities, along with opportunities for continuing professional development.

Among the many important initial training objectives are the following: understanding the nature and processes of learning from experience/experiential learning; selecting and adapting assessment methods; defining learning objectives; providing appropriate evaluations of outcomes through sound feedback techniques; enhancing the validity and reliability of assessment; and interpreting standards in awarding credit.

9.42 New assessors should be supervised and provided feedback regarding their evaluation of learning and credit awards. This helps ensure that they do not inadvertently set their own standards too low or too high in relation to institutional guidelines.

9.43 All persons involved in any aspect of the assessment process should be acquainted with relevant experiential learning provisions of the regional accrediting association and of any specialized accrediting bodies that may be involved.

9.44 Reward systems should be developed and evaluated for their effectiveness in creating a culture of high expectations for performance and continued development.

Principles and procedures related to Standard X:

"Assessment programs should be regularly monitored, reviewed, evaluated, and revised as needed to reflect changes in the needs being served, the purposes being met, and in the state of the assessment arts."

To keep quality assurance in the consciousness of everyone involved, it is essential for good assessment practice to have three characteristics: sound conception, effective implementation, and systematic program evaluation. The previous nine sections have been primarily concerned with the creation and implementation of assessment procedures. Quality assurance relies on the critical third characteristic—systematic program evaluation. This includes monitoring adherence to the program's or institution's rationale (Principle 7.1), exercising good practices, and improving effectiveness through continued learning. The more that systems for monitoring quality are embedded in the routine of assessment, the more likely it is that this standard will be met.

Foster professional standards

10.1 Standards of professional practice in assessment should be appropriate to the assessment method employed. In the assessment of experiential learning, it is especially important to foster a strong sense of collegial quality control as well as administrative responsibility.

10.11 An appropriate individual or group within the institution or organization should have clearly designated responsibility for monitoring the quality of assessment procedures.

10.12 The results of assessment should undergo systematic routine evaluation. This would include studying faculty interpretation of assessment policies and gauging consistency in the outcomes of assessment. This practice is a basic precept of quality assurance.

10.13 Periodic review of assessment procedures and of pertinent information should involve an objective and informed outsider as well as those who routinely participate in assessment.

One purpose of such review should be to note marked discrepancies between assessment policies or results and those of other institutions. The occurrence of such discrepancies should be an occasion for examining the rationale of institutional policies as well as the practices themselves.

10.14 Objective examinations and other standardized assessment instruments should be evaluated on the basis of empirical evidence regarding their reliability and validity. Such evidence constitutes a principal safeguard for ensuring quality and minimizing abuse. The corollary safeguard in expert judgment of experiential learning lies in faculty/assessor consensus regarding policy, peer review of practices, appropriate authentication of evidence, and systematic review of day-to-day program operation.

10.2 Periodic checks should be made to ensure that assessors are adhering to institutional assessment guidelines and procedures.

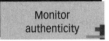
Seek agreement on practices

10.21 At regular intervals, it should be determined whether there is reasonable agreement regarding institutional policy on the standard of creditable learning, the extent to which there is adherence to this standard, and what learning is creditable against particular degree objectives. There is often substantial faculty disagreement in these areas, and it is common for institutional standards to fluctuate. Written guidelines, faculty development activities, and routine checks on agreement are necessary in order to achieve and maintain satisfactory consensus on such issues.

10.3 The authenticity of different types of documentation should be checked periodically.

Monitor authenticity

10.31 Students should be apprised of authentication procedures that might be applied to evidence of learning that they submit for review.

10.32 Periodic checks should be made to ensure that there is adequate faculty verification of documentation and student self-reports before credit is awarded.

10.4 Institutions should establish routine procedures for regularly examining the consistency of assessment judgments and credit awards.

Monitor consistency of assessments

Though reasonable consistency can be achieved when assessors subscribe to common principles and guidelines, adequate consistency should be verified in order to ensure that assessments are fair. The most dependable way to make such a verification is to undertake a special study in which the same assessment is carried out twice through usual procedures, and then the results are compared for consistency.

10.41 The results of these studies should inform judgments as to the adequacy of assessment procedures and the competence of assessors.

For example, analyses of assessment results should provide answers to questions such as the following: *(a)* Are any assessors consistently unable to agree reasonably well with other assessors? *(b)* Do assessment outcomes indicate that reasonably consistent agreement is seldom possible with respect to particular assessment methods or types of learning?

(c) Is there any indication that particular assessors or classes of assessors are consistently more or less lenient in applying standards and principles?

10.42 Particular assessors or methods of assessment should not be used if evidence indicates that assessment is not measuring what it is intended to, if assessments are frequently unreliable, or if some students do not appear to be fairly assessed.

Analyses of the degree of consistency between two independent sets of assessments should take into account the fact that a high level of agreement between judges can occur merely because both pass a similar percentage of students. There are typically two types of disagreement between assessors: Assessors can disagree on the standard they impose (i.e., what percent pass) or in the choice of which individual they judge to meet the standard. The latter is normally considered a much more dependable basis for deciding whether assessments are reasonably consistent.

Use appropriate technical procedures

10.5 Standard methods of measurement and statistics should be employed in evaluating the validity and reliability of experiential learning assessment procedures.

10.6 Periodic checks should be made to determine whether students believe that assessment procedures are sound and equitable and whether the institution is fulfilling satisfactorily the commitments made concerning experiential learning programs.

Monitor value to those affected by the assessment of learning

10.61 Special effort should be exerted to determine in what ways the assessment process could be made more beneficial to the student's self-development and self-awareness of personal competence. Whenever possible, it is desirable to evaluate alternate methods of assessment with these objectives in mind.

10.62 Efforts should also be made to determine the effectiveness of the learning assessment from perspectives outside of the institution (i.e., stakeholders' perceptions).

Implement periodic program evaluations

10.7 In addition to formative evaluation and improvement, experiential learning and related assessment efforts should undergo periodic summative evaluation of overall effectiveness, efficiency, and continuing usefulness in their current form.

10.71 Standards for measuring effectiveness should be articulated. They may not necessarily be the same as for teacher-directed activities.

Misconceptions, Poor Practices, and Issues

The primary focus of this book is on the standards and principles of assessment. The underlying premise is that good assessment practices are worthy of attention because of what they contribute to individual learning as well as personal, professional, and institutional development.

We have focused particular attention on learning from experience and experiential learning, which is an extraordinarily fertile area for further exploration. Assessment of experiential learning tests widely held assumptions and beliefs about the nature of learning and the relationship between learners, as students, and the institutions or organizations that serve as arbiters of creditable learning.

Establishing an assessment program entails a series of decisions. At any juncture, misconceptions, poor practices, and unresolved issues can challenge the system. Careful deliberation and consistent monitoring of assessment concepts and practices will enhance development and continuation of effective assessment programs. Lack of attention to values, assumptions, new information, standards, or theories of learning can actually lead to termination of existing programs or disapproval of requests for resources or of new proposals.

The purpose of this chapter is to highlight serious misconceptions that can lead to poor practices and to expose common poor practices. This chapter also raises some key issues that must be addressed in order to implement a successful program.

Misconceptions

1. Credit for prior learning is mainly a marketing tool to bolster adult enrollment.

Professionally responsible assessment of experiential learning certainly facilitates access and encourages enrollment. It is also true that older students, who are more likely to have more creditable experiential learning than younger ones, seek recognition and credit for their experiential learning and thus avoid redundant learning. But these reasons are not enough to attract adult learners if the educational programs are not adult friendly in other ways as well, such as curricula responsive to adult needs and interests, teaching that is responsive to the ways in which adults are likely to learn most effectively, and administrative services that are respectful of adults' busy lives. Credit for prior learning is likely to enhance adult enrollment when it is part of an adult-oriented system.

2. Portfolio-based documentation processes, while still suspect in some quarters, are preferable to other forms of evidence for the assessment of learning gained through experience.

Portfolios and other forms of documentation have many attractive features. Portfolios bring together disparate strands of "learning data" to be reflected upon and compiled into direct and indirect evidence of learning to be measured and evaluated. In addition, preparing the portfolio and undergoing evaluation early in a program provides students with a clearer sense of remaining degree requirements.[13]

However, it is a misconception to judge one form of documentation as better than another. The best forms of documentation make the learning assessable. The realization of this principle, then, rests on the clarity of the expected learning outcomes and the criteria to be applied to measure the level of learning. These factors set the context for deciding what appropriate forms of evidence may look like, from examinations to performance in simulations to testimonies or observations of applied learning in live contexts to portfolios.

3. It is improper to offer both credit and pay for experiential learning that takes place on the job.

This misconception often accompanies the discussion of internships, cooperative education assignments, and other work-and-learn programs. The source of this misunderstanding is the common confusion between experiential activities and learning outcomes. In fact, payment or compensation is primarily given for the activity, while credit is awarded for the outcome. The experiential activity for which the employer pays is an input; the learning gained from the experience(s) for which credit or other credentialing may be awarded is an outcome.

---

[13] For a discussion of portfolios and various strategies for their use, see Elana Michelson, Alan Mandell, and contributors, *Portfolio Development and the Assessment of Prior Learning: Perspectives, Models, and Practices* (Sterling, VA: Stylus Publishing, 2004).

The evaluation of learning and the award of credit are processes separate from the acquisition of learning, just as they are in a classroom. In experiential learning, it doesn't make sense to differentiate between the learning of volunteers and the learning of paid workers if a valid assessment indicates that they have learned the same thing, unless the learning objectives involve something about the nature of volunteering itself.

4. Only courses taken on campus should be accepted for residence credit.

A policy requiring a fixed proportion of credits to be earned in residence is based on two assumptions: first, that campus-based courses always have some added value as they are taken within a community of scholars and, second, that learning acquired elsewhere does not provide this advantage. If the institution can demonstrate that learning outcomes are more aligned with its criteria for quality when the learning occurs in residence, then these assumptions are obviously validated. However, the premise that there is something special to be gained from immersion in a community of scholars is difficult to defend on commuter campuses. Many working students rush onto campus just before class and depart immediately afterward. If it is the presumption of quality assurance for teacher-directed education that underscores the residency requirement, unless the same assurance holds for the assessment of the learning outcomes, this comes close to equating input with the defining element of a quality residence-based education. The rapid infusion of distance-based education programs of many kinds—from degree-granting to certificate-offering to credentialing programs—is perhaps the ultimate challenge to defining the meaning of residence and its importance to policy formation.

Besides, it isn't necessarily accurate to conclude that the experiential learner was totally denied the advantages of a community of scholars. With the highly mobile community of contemporary life, scholars are found in the workplace, at dinner parties, in the family, and in the media (including on the Internet). It is certainly the case that the structure and organization of the learning can differ significantly when it occurs on a college campus and that there is more opportunity for informal participation in a community of scholars in a resident situation. However, without describing the advantage of a residency in terms of the learning outcomes, it is quite difficult to justify the residency requirement. Where learning takes place and how it takes place are not necessarily equivalent. The more experience-based learning is developed as an intended objective of education, the more likely residency arguments are to find a footing—or not—in the realities of contemporary life.

5. Credit for experiential learning should not be granted at the graduate level.

Opposition or resistance to granting graduate-level credit to learning from experience comes in several forms—concern for quality assurance, the belief that graduate learning is somehow so different that it cannot be attained anywhere except in graduate school or postbaccalaureate credentialing programs, and concern over decreased enrollment if the practice were to become widespread.

Actually, each of these sources of opposition is frequently belied by the actual practices of most graduate schools. While there may be resistance to the idea of granting credit for external learning, it is already going on under a different name, in the form of waivers, substitutions, and alternate methods of satisfying requirements. Each of these practices takes into account prior learning. What results is a respect for not requiring repetitive learning, but this is handled as a change in the requirements, not a reduction of them. A graduate degree under these conceptions can be considered value added in contrast to a chronicle of competence.

As with so many other misconceptions about the role assessment can play in the design of education, if graduate as well as undergraduate degrees were defined in terms of learning outputs—demonstrable competence in specified knowledge and skills—the overemphasis on inputs might be diminished and the meaning of a degree would align more closely with a conception of generally acceptable evidence of specified levels and amounts of learning.

6. Awarding advanced placement without credit and waiving requirements are reasonable alternatives to awarding credit for prior experiential learning.

This is related to the previous misconception. It is more common in undergraduate education, however, to waive requirements without credit and replace them with the expectation of additional course work. For example, students with demonstrable competence in a foreign language may be placed in advanced classes but denied credit for their competence. This results in a value added but distorted meaning of a baccalaureate degree. The student with the equivalent learning of, say, six credit units still must make up those six units by taking additional electives. The student ends up overfulfilling the requirements, reaching the same level of competence that is required of all students in the foreign language area, and completing six more credit units than other students. Again, the misconception underlying this practice is that a degree depends on the amount of time spent rather than on the learning outcomes achieved.

Poor Practices
1. Granting credit for experience, not learning.
This is grievous enough to be considered malpractice. It is the essence of Standard I and the persistent theme throughout this book. It is highlighted here because the practice still exists. The granting of credit or a credential on the basis of time served, rather than on learning outcomes achieved, is a major violation of good assessment practices.

2. Basing assessment fees on the number of credits awarded.
This is a direct violation of Standard VIII. When credits are awarded for fees, two serious negative results occur: It inaccurately reflects the true costs of assessment, and it injects a profit motive into a decision that should be made only on academic grounds. The real cost of assessment may be the same for a "no credit" decision as for a more positive finding. It may make sense to set fees in terms of units assessed, but not in terms of units awarded.

The negative influence of a profit motivation can be either personal or institutional. It is probably most important for for-profit institutions to pay particular attention to this, though not-for-profit institutions can be just as prone to place revenue above good practices. On the individual side, this practice can be a problem when the assessor's compensation is dependent on the number of units granted.

The only way to ensure quality in the award of academic or credentialing credit is to ensure that the charges for assessment are, in fact, based on the cost of assessment and not the award of credit.

3. Promising that credit is likely to be awarded.
Even in institutions and programs where substantial care is taken to grant credit for learning, not experience, a careless approach to advertising often implies that a credit award is likely. Once a prospective student's expectations have been raised by catchy World Wide Web ads or brochures with statements such as "Your life experience can earn college credit," assessors may find themselves on the defensive and have a difficult time enforcing the standards.

It is not an easy process to prepare a portfolio or evidence of learning. Good practice requires that materials on learning assessment state the following facts: Credit is only granted for learning; an applicant for credit is expected to invest significant time and effort in making the case that experience has, in fact, resulted in creditable learning; it is not possible to know in advance whether (or, if so, how much) credit may be awarded; and the final determination of credit or credentialing awards will be based on expert measurement and evaluation of that learning.

4. Judging learning from experience too early in the assessment process is likely to negate the deserved award of credit or a credential.

The early steps of the process for assessing learning gained through reflection on experience can be truncated by a premature judgment by an advisor or mentor to the process that a given area of learning is not going to be awarded credit. This is the flipside of the poor practice of implicitly promising credit for experience just described. The identification step should be a patient exploration of the possibilities. It is certainly realistic to expect an experienced advisor to anticipate that some claims to learning by a student may indeed never see the awarding of credit or a credential. However, students new to the process of PLA often first need time and space to surface and describe significant events in their lives before they can articulate their learning at a level of detail and depth that will ultimately be required for documentation and evaluation. Inhibiting the mining of the possibilities by derailing the process prematurely may miss surfacing a student's tacit knowledge. It is also likely to inhibit students from trying again at a future date to bring forth creditable learning, even though it may very well be present.

5. Involving incompetent persons in assessment and evaluation.

Standard IV states that persons responsible for assessing and evaluating the learning must have relevant expertise in the subject matter *content* and in the assessment process. These two types of expertise are required for determining levels of competence and awarding credit. It is certainly possible to find individuals who embody both kinds of expertise. Full-time, regularly appointed faculty certainly should possess both content and process expertise in their areas of specialization. Experiential learning, however, crosses boundaries of both disciplines and place, and requires individualized assessment. A single faculty member may be qualified in part of the content and in part of the appropriate assessment procedure, but not necessarily all of both. More than one assessor may be needed for a sound assessment. Further, a qualified assessor might not be a member of the full-time faculty but someone who, by virtue of her/his applied knowledge and relevant context, can determine the academic or professional meaning of a student's learning and value of a particular competence. Institutions may be tempted to save money, time, or effort by relying on insufficiently prepared assessors or by limiting assessment to certain areas of knowledge that reside in the faculty, rather than including experts from the wider community.

Once the assessment process is underway, incompetent assessment is sometimes the result of misguided, though sincere, attempts to be objective, such as by avoiding contact between the assessor and the learner. While the virtues of anonymity are realized, the advantages of probing through personal contact are lost. The assessment deficiency that results may be in either direction: the award of credit that is not deserved; or the failure to uncover and give appropriate credit for learning that the isolated petitioner did not himself/herself recognize or report in the proper manner.

As assessment processes become institutionalized, approaches (e.g., portfolio) can become mechanized; specific measurable parts supercede the gestalt; or the details overshadow important generic capabilities. Credentialing by regulatory authorities or institutions with expanding and large enrollment is probably most susceptible to these pitfalls of making routine a process that by its very nature has strong elements of individualization.

6. Granting credit for progress rather than for attaining learning that meets the agreed upon criteria.

This is a common practice in some academic cultures. It is possible, of course, for someone to expend considerable effort and make a great deal of progress but still not achieve a level of competence that is appropriate for the credit or credential. What makes this troublesome practice difficult to eliminate is that effort and progress are thoroughly commendable learning objectives. It is difficult to argue against a vision of education in which all individuals learn all that is possible and appropriate for them to learn, taking into account where they started and how far they are capable of going. What amounts to poor assessment practice, however, is to confuse effort and progress with achievement of creditable levels of competence. Summative evaluations (i.e., grades) lose meaning or credibility if grading or other summative judgments are based on progress and not achievement, unless the criteria for doing so are agreed upon and public.

7. Restricting the assessment of experiential learning for credit to only certain areas of a curriculum without a clear rationale.

It is common for programs to allow credit by assessment of prior learning in some areas of the curriculum and not others. Some programs do not allow credit for experiential learning in the major but do allow it in general education areas or vice versa. It is the prerogative, of course, of any program or institution to insist on participation in the community of scholars that constitute the faculty in a particular segment of offerings. Residency requirements raise the question of whether the learning outcomes do, in fact, differ for in-residence learners and experientially based learners. Without a clear rationale for their policies, programs and institutions often send a mixed message regarding their commitment to criteria-based assessment.

Anticipated Issues

When establishing a sound assessment program with well-prepared assessors, numerous issues will arise, many of which may be anticipated. Assessment entails a series of decisions, guided by standards and principles and open to interpretations based on mission, values, philosophies of learning or education, and degrees of knowledge about assessment and evaluation processes. Predictably, issues lurking below the surface of an institution or organization often come to the surface during assessment.

We've selected just four issues for which, like any good issue, there are multiple perspectives that form sides from which to derive a resolution, at least until there is sufficient unrest to revisit the issue again. The standards and principles can help frame the arguments that the issues can generate, although they don't offer codified solutions.

How is individual learning recognized within collaborative learning contexts?

There is little argument that contemporary work and community life demands collaborative and cooperative capabilities. The collective achievement of goals inevitably leads to a degree of shared knowledge and learning that may not reside solely in one individual. Academic achievement, however, is often viewed as an individual accomplishment based on the belief that each person is accountable for what he/she has learned. Without even challenging this tenet, an assessment question emerges of no small proportion: How does one fairly and appropriately assess a person's competency when it has been developed with others and to meet goals not connected explicitly to the academic enterprise?

Who is excluded by assessment policies and practices?

The concept of variation and individual differences in learning preferences and strategies is widely accepted and respected in the areas of teaching and learning. With regard to assessment, however, attention to individual differences hasn't reached the same level of consideration. Physical limitations, preferences for expression of knowledge in media other than text, the extent to which emotional intelligence is converted to affective knowing, and a host of other ways to describe and analyze learning outcomes expand or limit the scope of the assessment capabilities of any program or individual assessor. Consequently, policies that assume some forms of assessment are more appropriate—not necessarily more valid—than others necessarily exclude some portion of most populations. How responsive to individual differences should assessment policies and practices be?

What financial model best supports an assessment program: self-sustaining or subsidized?

The ultimate goal of most institutions would be to establish an assessment program that holds itself accountable, generates resources for improvements and growth, and is self-sustaining so that it is not susceptible to reduction of resources or changes in administration. Another incentive for a self-sustaining model is that assessment can be built into faculty load. Over the long run, expecting faculty to carry out the tasks of assessment without reducing their course load can erode an assessment program that is successful in all other ways.

The expenses of a quality assessment program include salaries and honoraria, space, professional development, and materials, along with shared costs such as physical plant and administrative services (e.g., transcription). A key step on the road to being self-sustaining is to segregate all the functions associated with the assessment process and determine the costs for each. Students should be responsible for the basic costs of assessment (which can be done reasonably, especially when they do not pay for assessment by the credit [see Standard VIII]). The principal assumption here is that the cost of assessment alone should be less than the cost of assessment when it is linked to instruction, which is the norm in classroom-based education.

Since assessment is rarely viewed as a central function of an educational enterprise, decisions about financing assessment efforts can translate into important, but differing, strategic outcomes—short- and long-term. It doesn't take a detailed analysis to draw a correlation between the complexity of assessment measures and the costs incurred by their development, implementation, and associated quality-assurance measures. Following is an illustration of the spectrum of assessment measures that could—and probably should—form the inventory of a well-developed assessment program:

- Performance
- Simulation
- Interview/dialogue (w/assessor)
- Tangible product (e.g., work based)
- Testimony from qualified observers
- Subject-based essay
- Standardized exam (e.g., CLEP, "local" challenge exam)
- Self-assessment

None of these is necessarily used alone, and several are often combined in practice. Yet it is likely that a majority of programs limit both their repertoires and their invitations to measure students' learning to the middle of the group—essays, standardized exams, and work products. And though there is not a recent survey of the measures education providers draw on, it is likely that associated costs are as much or more a factor in this decision as assessment philosophy. What financial models should be applied to the establishment, maintenance, and expansion of the capacity of a quality assessment program?

How does online learning change the face of assessment?

In most aspects, the standards and related principles should provide sufficient touchstones for assessment efforts, whether the relationships between institution and students are campus based or mediated by electronic media, such as the Internet (e.g., World Wide Web, e-mail). At this point in the evolution of digitized, distant relationships, there are two major issues regarding online assessment programs.

The first issue concerns the range and means of evidencing learning that is available for students. Even more than campus-based programs, online assessment privileges text—that is, it tends to limit students to visual representations of what they know. Incorporating aural (auditory) and kinesthetic modalities for online assessment is a challenge of the future. Also, the anonymity that is tempting but not necessary in campus-based relationships is more likely to be the norm in online programs.

The second issue concerns authenticity of students' work. How do we know for sure that the work submitted was actually created by the student? Assessment interactions, in large measure, rely on good faith and at least a basic level of trust in the honesty of all parties. Do the same presuppositions hold true for online assessment as for campus based, or does online, by its very nature, require a revaluation of them?

The emergence of technology to both store and retrieve information and documents as well as mediate communications is bringing with it opportunities to lower some of the costs of assessments and increase efficiencies as well as access for all parties involved. Some interactions currently done face-to-face may be replaced by asynchronous communications at a distance; in turn, experience with asynchronous communications may highlight those interactions that really are better carried out by direct, person-to-person interactions with skilled personnel.

In Conclusion

Misconceptions, poor practices, and issues that lead to unanticipated decision making can impede the development of sound assessment programs that respect and promote learning from experience. But they can also endanger the quality of assessment and evaluation in traditional programs as well.

Adherence to the ten standards and the principles and procedures of chapters 4, 5, and 6 can go a long way toward helping organizations, colleges, and universities meet acceptable, if not high, standards of quality. At the least, the conversation that ensues can lead to a variety of desirable outcomes, from heightened awareness of the criteria for quality assessment to the application of good assessment practices for individual and organizational improvement.

Glossary of Terms Associated with Prior Learning Assessment

Abbreviations for Prior Learning Assessment

APCL Assessment of Prior Certificated Learning (U.K.)

APEL Assessment of Prior Experiential Learning (Ireland, U.K., U.S.)

APL Assessment of Prior Learning (U.K.)

EVC Erkennen Vanelders of Informed Verworven Competenties (Netherlands)

PLA Prior Learning Assessment (U.S., Canada)

PLAR Prior Learning Assessment and Recognition (Canada)

RDA Reconnaissance des Acquis (Canada)

RPL Recognition of Prior Learning (Australia, South Africa, New Zealand)

Articulation

1. An agreement or set of agreements between institutions or programs that compares courses and specifies equivalencies; the agreements are most often based on intended outcomes, coverage of subject matter, or credits.

2. On an individual basis, the relationship of a person's learning being assessed for credit to academic, personal, or professional goals.

Assessment

The measurement of learning based on criteria and indicators.

Assessment Evidence

(See also Evidence of Learning.)
A product, artifact, or means by which individuals demonstrate their learning or capabilities that are amenable to public review and assessment (e.g., portfolio, demonstration, exam, simulation, or presentation).

Assessor

An individual with appropriate knowledge and skill who is responsible for measuring a person's learning.

Block Credit Model

The assignment of a variable number of credits to an individual's assessed evidence of learning based on a judgment of its breadth and depth as well as its relationship to the existing curriculum of the institution.

Certificate

An artifact or document verifying participation in training or another organized learning experience. Certificates may represent levels of that participation, ranging from only attendance to attendance with assessment of the desired learning outcomes.

Challenge Exam

A test of an individual's learning that is based on the expected outcomes of a course (or set of courses) in an institution's curriculum.

College-Level Learning

A standard set by a postsecondary institution to define the level of learning worthy of credit. Academia has used several definitions of college-level learning (e.g., a mix of theory and application or ideas and their application; the integration and interpretation of one's experiences using accepted ideas or theories; complexity of cognitive, perceptual, and behavioral dimensions of learning).

In response to the multiple sources and circumstances in which creditable learning can occur, several options have been used for determining college level in the assessment of prior learning, for example:

- relating the content of learning to subject areas traditionally taught in colleges;
- showing that what was learned is at a level of achievement equal to what is commonly recognized by (other) colleges;
- comparing specific learning to that acquired in college-level curricula;
- relating learning to a personal goal that requires college-level learning;
- identifying learning as that acquired after high school and expected for professional acceptance.

Competence

A demonstrable capability based on specific knowledge within a certain context.

Competence-Based Credit Model

The assignment of credit to demonstrated and assessed competence rather than to a specific body of knowledge or subject matter.

Course Challenge

A request for credit based on the demonstration of knowledge, specified learning outcomes, or competence equivalent to an existing course in a curriculum.

Course Equivalence Credit Model

The assignment of credit only for the demonstration of knowledge or learning equivalent to an existing course with a specified number of associated credits in a curriculum.

Credit

The value an institution attaches to a formal course of instruction. In the United States, a credit has usually been defined as 7.5 hours (in a quarter system) or 11 to 12 hours (on a semester schedule) of contact time between a faculty member and a student; however, the standards and definition may vary from institution to institution. Credit generally represents the academic legitimacy of assessed learning and contact time.

Credit Bank

An agency that allows individuals to bank evidence of academic or professional achievement; this allows an individual to accumulate credit from a variety of sources over an extended period of time in a single repository. The Open Learning Agency in Canada offers this service, for example.

Criteria

An articulated set of specifications by which someone's learning (or evidence of learning) may be measured and evaluated. Assessment criteria often cover variables such as authenticity, sufficiency, and currency of learning; the effectiveness of a criterion is measured by both its validity (Is it useful in measuring what it intends to provide guidelines for measuring?) and reliability (Would subsequent assessments of the same evidence produce similar results?).

Distance Education

(Also called *distributed education* or *distance learning*.)
The engagement in an educational activity when the learner is studying at a distance from the source of instruction; frequently, and in contrast to face-to-face situations, the distance between learner and instructor is accompanied by asynchronicity (i.e., communications are separated by time as well as physical space). Increasingly, this form of education is mediated and aided by various forms of both communication and storage technology.

Evidence of Learning

(See also Assessment Evidence.)
Documents, artifacts, or other products that represent what a person knows or can do (i.e., has learned) and that are used to substantiate an individual's claim for credit in an assessment process. Evidence may be direct (what the person says or represents regarding his/her learning) or indirect (what others say about the learning).

Evaluation

The determination of the quality of an individual's learning relative to standards.

Experiential Learning

Learning that has been gained as a result of reflecting upon the events or experiences in one's life in contrast to formal education.

Feedback

Commentary offered to an individual that addresses the quality of the evidence submitted for assessment. Some of the qualities of feedback are clarity, integrity (with respect to public criteria), flexibility (in the recognition of various expressions of learning), empathy (in the communication style), and timeliness.

Goal(s) Statement

One of the components of a portfolio or other evidence presented for assessment for credit. The intent of a goals statement is to help individuals in the prior learning assessment process clarify their short- and long-term personal, professional, or educational goals to set a context for the assessment process.

Learning from Experience

A process by which individuals may determine what they have identified as meaningful and potentially creditable from the events and experiences of their lives.

Learning Outcome

A statement of measurable (or anticipated) learning that describes what a person should know and/or be able to do as a result of a (formal or informal) learning experience.

Letter of Testimony

A letter or document prepared by someone who is appropriately qualified to substantiate a person's claim of knowledge or skills because of direct observation of that person. Letters of testimony often constitute some or all of the evidence of learning in an individual's request for credit in an assessment process.

Lifelong Learning

As a noun, this is the learning gained in both formal and informal situations that people accumulate over the course of their lives. As a verb, it is the process(es) of gaining knowledge in formal and informal situations (i.e., the full range of life's experiences).

Measurement of Learning

One of the steps in a prior learning assessment process that entails determining the degree and level of learning an individual has achieved.

Mentoring

The process of helping someone else develop their own skills, knowledge, attitudes, and/or values through various strategies, including modeling of these attributes, advising, coaching, and promoting other activities that contribute to advancing the person's capabilities and capacities. In an assessment process, mentoring may serve as an important bridge between identifying creditable learning and articulating the appropriate evidence for its assessment and measurement.

Nonsponsored Learning

(See Unsponsored Learning.)

Open Learning

A philosophy of education that increases access to education so that anyone can study anything at any place and at any time is called *open learning*. An institution that supports open learning is usually characterized by open or flexible admissions policies, flexible start and completion dates, courses offered via a variety of media and methodologies, recognition of credentials from other institutions or sources, and recognition of the learning from experience and lifelong learning.

Open Learning Agency

A publicly funded organization in British Columbia, Canada, that has a specialty in the delivery of distance education and training; the agency coordinates its activities with industries, government, and educational partners.

Portfolio

A collection of evidence in support of a person's claim for credit through a prior learning assessment process.

Portfolio Development

The process of identifying and creating documentation or other evidence of learning to be organized for presentation in support of a claim(s) for credit via a prior learning assessment process. In some programs or institutions, the portfolio development is assisted by a course to structure a step-by-step process.

Prerequisite

A requirement—often a course or program (or its equivalent)—that must be successfully completed by an assessment process before participating or enrolling in an advanced course or program.

Principles of Assessment

The standards and guidelines that guide the processes, activities, and quality assurance of the processes for measuring and evaluating learning.

Prior Learning Assessment (PLA)

(See also Abbreviations for Prior Learning Assessment.)
A process by which an individual's learning from experience is assessed and evaluated for purposes of granting credit, certification, or advanced standing toward further education or training.

Quality Assurance

Efforts and associated processes to ensure that standards are being met.

Reflection/Reflective Thought

A wide range of processes for identifying, reviewing, interpreting, and deriving meaning or meaningful learning from one's experiences.

Residency Requirement

A minimum number of credits an institution requires of students to be awarded a credential, such as a degree, from that institution.

Self-assessment

An activity and process by which an individual describes and judges the nature, extent, and level of one's own learning or performance, self-assessment is a component of reflection and it is often a part of, or an outcome of a prior learning assessment process.

Self-directed Learning

The type of learning in which an individual takes responsibility for identifying, goal setting, managing, and assessing or seeking assessment, self-directed learning does not mean learning alone because one may choose the strategies for learning collaboratively or in structured situations as an option for directing their learning.

Skill Set

A grouping of complementary skills that constitute a larger or more abstract role—for example, the skill set for a manager may include communications, performance evaluation, expertise of the industry, analytic and systemic thinking, and interpersonal abilities.

Sponsored Learning

Preplanned learning experiences offered by a postsecondary institution.

Transcript

The formal record of a student's achievement in an academic institution or certification program.

Transfer Credit

The recognition of credits earned in one institution by another institution.

Transferable Skills

Knowledge, capabilities, attitudes, or values that are effective across multiple contexts, such as various workplaces or organizations.

Unsponsored Learning

(Also called *nonformal learning*.) Organized events or unplanned results of life or work experiences; skills and knowledge gained through unstructured events and experiences.

APPENDIX

B Steps and Principles for Assessing Sponsored Experiential Learning

Step 1. ARTICULATION: Relate learning goals to academic, personal, and professional goals
  1.1 Determine what is creditable
  1.2 Define criteria for acceptable standards of learning
  1.3 Define learner's rationale or general purpose(s) for seeking the learning objectives
    1.31 Encourage self-awareness and personal development
    1.32 Encourage student design of learning objectives
  1.4 To the extent possible, coordinate goals with the learning environment

Step 2. PLANNING: Select appropriate learning objectives and activities
  2.1 Determine the standards and associated criteria for the acceptable level of learning
  2.2 Develop a learning plan
    2.21 Express outcomes in terms of competencies
    2.22 Select learning activities in anticipation of evaluation
    2.23 Respect and account for individual differences in learning strategies, preferences, and styles in the planning of learning activities
  2.3 Emphasize learner's role in preparing for sponsored experiential learning
    2.31 Orient to the learning environment
  2.4 Bridge the planning and evaluation steps (e.g., through learning contracts)

Step 3. EVALUATION: Determine the credit equivalency
  3.1 Decide who categorizes and defines competencies
  3.2 Define evaluation criteria and make them public
    3.21 Define levels of competence, using criteria and examples
  3.3 Measure outcomes, not inputs
  3.4 Use same or comparable standards for measuring teacher-directed and experiential learning outcomes

3.41 State the basis for translating outcomes into credit hours or credentialing thresholds

3.5 Credit or recognize learning, not experience

3.51 Precede new learning with a review of prior learning

3.52 Provide frequent feedback on progress toward learning objectives during learning activities

3.53 Integrate evaluation into planning and program

Step 4. DOCUMENTATION: Create and organize evidence of learning

4.1 Develop an institutional policy(ies) regarding documentation

4.2 Specify appropriate documentation

4.21 Include various uses of documentation in the guidelines for documentation

4.3 Documentation should distinguish experience from learning

4.31 Provide evidence of learning along with descriptions of learning

4.4 Authenticate and qualify evidence

4.41 Establish procedures for authentication of electronically communicated evidence that represent a combination of appropriate technology and the values of the organization

4.42 Provide guidelines for documentation by testimony

4.43 Require that supporting testimonies as evidence address the extent and level of learning, not recommendations for credit award

4.5 Emphasize and reward quality, not quantity

Step 5. MEASUREMENT: Determine the degree and level of learning/ competence achieved

5.1 Fit assessment methods to the learning

5.2 Fit assessment methods to the learner

5.3 Use assessment as a part of learning

5.4 Ensure reliability

5.41 Use more than one sample of evidence when possible

5.42 Use more than one assessor

5.43 Avoid various forms of bias, discrimination, or unconscious error in judging performance or work

5.5 Ensure validity

5.51 Assess learning by comparing to learning objectives

5.52 Use more than one method of assessment

5.6 Train assessors; seek training as an assessor
    5.61 Provide written guidelines and training materials for assessors (and seek them out)
    5.62 Match assessment training to assessment method
    5.63 Maintain consistent conditions
5.7 State results; provide feedback
5.8 Encourage and develop self-assessment skills
    5.81 Involve learner in assessment process

Step 6. TRANSCRIPTION: Prepare a useful record of results
6.1 Communicate with third parties
    6.11 Establish panels for review of narrative transcripts
    6.12 Describe learning outcomes clearly
6.2 Record learning appropriately
    6.21 Find alternatives to misleading course labels
    6.22 Reference specific criteria or syllabi in course labels
    6.23 Describe learning outcomes
6.3 Describe content and level of learning
    6.31 Identify the learning environment
    6.32 Include significant details

Steps and Principles for Assessing Unsponsored, Prior Experiential Learning

Step 1. IDENTIFICATION: Review experience to identify learning that is potentially creditable or appropriate for credentialing
  1.1 Develop strategies for describing learning experiences
  1.2 Differentiate between learning and experience
  1.3 Specify learning outcomes
      1.31 Allow sufficient time and patience to arrive at specific learning outcomes
  1.4 Use assessment to promote and reinforce learning
  1.5 Facilitate reentry into an academic culture and future learning
      1.51 Provide guidance, printed materials
      1.52 Institute a formal structure for helping people to identify possible creditable learning
Step 2. ARTICULATION: Relate proposed credit to academic, personal, and professional goals
  2.1 Determine what is creditable
  2.2 Align the articulation with criteria for acceptable level of learning outcomes
      2.21 Note issues for later attention
  2.3 Relate proposed creditable learning to program objectives
      2.31 Create a process to help learners articulate their learning, personal goals, and program goals
      2.32 Enhance learner self-awareness through the articulation process
  2.4 Consider the recency of learning
Step 3. DOCUMENTATION: Prepare evidence to support claim for credit
  3.1 Make sure assessment is based on evidence
      3.11 Formulate policies regarding the role(s) of documentation
  3.2 Documentation should reference what is creditable learning
  3.3 Develop perspectives and policies on primary and secondary forms of evidence and documentation

3.31 Specify appropriate types of documentation

3.32 Provide examples of various types of documentation

3.33 Determine and make public the appropriate uses of documentation

3.34 Communicate that learning is experiential

3.4 Authenticate evidence

3.41 Create procedures for authentication of electronically submitted evidence

3.42 Request that testimony documentation addresses the learning outcomes and establishes the qualifications of the individual to represent an individual's learning

3.43 Request that secondary documentation address learning outcomes, not qualities of the learner per se

3.5 Judge quality of evidence, not quantity

3.6 Make documentation contribute to learning

Step 4. MEASUREMENT: Determine the degree and level of learning/competence achieved

4.1 Fit assessment method to the learning

4.2 Fit assessment methods to the learner

4.3 Measure outcomes, not inputs

4.4 Utilize assessment as learning

4.41 Develop and practice assessment methods that promote further learning

4.5 Ensure reliability

4.51 Use more than one sample of evidence when possible

4.52 Use more than one assessor

4.53 Avoid various forms of bias, discrimination, or unconscious error in judging a student's work or performance

4.6 Ensure validity

4.61 Assess learning by comparing to learning objectives

4.62 Seek different forms of evidence of learning; use more than one type of assessment

4.7 Train assessors; seek training as an assessor

4.71 Written guidelines and training materials should be available and sought out by assessors

4.72 Match assessment training to assessment method

4.73 Maintain consistent conditions

4.8 State results; provide feedback

4.9 Encourage and develop self-assessment skills

    4.91 Have learners participate in the design and administration of assessment process

Step 5. EVALUATION: Determine the credit equivalency

  5.1 Decide who categorizes and defines competencies

  5.2 Maintain integrity and equity by making criteria public

    5.21 Evaluate an individual's learning in relation to public criteria

    5.22 Employ subject matter and assessment expertise

    5.23 Relate criteria for crediting or credentialing learning to institutional goals and character

  5.3 Provide a clear and rational basis for awarding credit for learning from experience

    5.31 Adopt and justify the credit model appropriate for the institution and the outcomes of learning

    5.32 Rationalize any limits to the amount of learning that can be credited

    5.33 Specify basis for translating assessed outcomes into credit hours or credentialing thresholds

    5.34 Consider accommodation of partial credits for assessed outcomes

  5.4 Establish the same or comparable standards for measuring teacher-directed and experiential learning outcomes

    5.41 Specify basis for translating assessed outcomes into credit hours or credentialing thresholds

  5.5 Credit or recognize learning, not experience; outcomes, not inputs

  5.6 Provide useful feedback

    5.61 Establish guidelines for the quality and characteristics of good feedback

    5.62 Precede each new major learning activity with a review of prior learning

    5.63 Provide summative feedback as soon as possible following an assessment

    5.64 Follow the assignment of credits for assessed learning with advice on implications for degree or credential requirements

    5.65 Extend advising on the outcomes of an assessment to include plans for future learning

5.7 Consider alternative forms of recognition for assessed experiential learning

    5.71 Provide options for partial credit that may also be sufficient as prerequisite credit

5.8 Provide for review and appeal

    5.81 Treat review of individual assessments as part of a comprehensive program review

5.9 Avoid awarding of duplicate credit

Step 6. TRANSCRIPTION: Prepare a useful record of results

    6.1 Communicate with third parties

        6.11 Succinctly describe individual learning

        6.12 Retain the functions of a transcript while recording learning outcomes

        6.13 Establish panels for review of narrative transcripts

    6.2 Set policies regarding transcripts

        6.21 Provide information that validates and legitimizes assessed learning

    6.3 Record learning appropriately

        6.31 Find alternatives to misleading course labels

        6.32 Describe learning outcomes, not experiences

Administrative Measures to Ensure Quality Principles and Procedures Related to Standards VII–X

Publish Policies and Procedures

Standard VII: Policies and procedures applied to assessment, including provision for appeal, should be fully disclosed and prominently available to all parties involved in the assessment process.

7.1   Articulate a rationale for assessment policies
     7.11   Support decision making with a clear rationale
7.2   Create a clear process for review and change of policies
     7.21   Create levels of review such that each level contributes to the quality of the decision making
7.3   Derive policies and practices from an integrated curriculum
     7.31   Determine what experiential learning is effective in completing curriculum requirements
     7.32   Clarify how assessment and experiential learning function in relation to other components of the curriculum and institution/organization
     7.33   Develop an operational model for assessment and experiential learning
7.4   Clarify roles and responsibilities
7.5   Create a centralized source (handbook) of policies, procedures, roles, and responsibilities
     7.51   Include all elements of an assessment program
     7.52   Provide the same handbook to professional personnel and students
     7.53   Ensure "truth in advertising"
7.6   Protect individual privacy
7.7   Determine perspectives and policies regarding individual differences

Develop Appropriate Fee Schedules

Standard VIII: Fees charged for assessment should be based on the services performed in the process and not determined by the amount of credit awarded.

8.1 Charge fees for assessment, not for credit
    8.11 Make clear what services will be provided for an assessment fee
    8.12 Make fees proportional to the amount of anticipated assessment effort
    8.13 Establish fees independent of the assessment outcome
8.2 Ensure cost-effectiveness
    8.21 Ensure equitable fees for students and pay for faculty
8.3 Recognize assessment as a contribution to learning
    8.31 Remunerate assessors on the basis of expertise and effort, not credit hours awarded
8.4 Monitor cost-effectiveness and efficiency
    8.41 Establish prices that are equitable in relation to actual cost of assessment and the real benefit of the assessment process itself

Professional Development Is a Reciprocal Responsibility

Standard IX: All personnel involved in the assessment of learning should pursue and receive adequate training and continuing professional development for the functions they perform.

9.1 Identify who can and should participate in the assessment process and clarify their respective roles
    9.11 Create a rationale for who is included in and excluded from an assessment process
    9.12 Establish qualifications of assessors
9.2 Determine the number of assessors who should evaluate an individual's learning
9.3 Specify responsibilities of assessors and associated personnel
    9.31 Design training to meet the responsibilities
    9.32 Expect an understanding of both the broad and technical aspects of assessment
    9.33 Use assessors who have knowledge of both their specialty and general assessment

9.4   Create a culture to ensure quality through continued learning
  9.41   Provide training and ongoing professional development to everyone connected with assessment
  9.42   Provide feedback to new assessors
  9.43   Inform assessment personnel about accreditation rules
  9.44   Set high expectations and reward performance

Evaluate Experiential Learning Programs

Standard X: Assessment programs should be regularly monitored, reviewed, evaluated, and revised as needed to reflect changes in the needs being served, the purposes being met, and in the state of the assessment arts.

10.1   Foster professional standards
  10.11   Designate review personnel
  10.12   Study the results of reviews; identify areas for resolution of differences
  10.13   Involve outside reviewers
  10.14   Evaluate assessment methods and strategies
10.2   Seek agreement on practices
  10.21   Periodically check on levels of agreement among personnel regarding policies and practices
10.3   Monitor authenticity
  10.31   Inform students of authenticity procedures
  10.32   Periodically check on assessor verification of documentation and authenticity of self-reports
10.4   Monitor consistency of assessment
  10.41   Use periodic review to evaluate quality of assessment procedures
  10.42   Discontinue involvement of unreliable assessors and methods
10.5   Use appropriate technical procedures
10.6   Monitor value of assessment to those affected by it
  10.61   Select assessment methods that maximize learning and development of learners
  10.62   Assess value and quality of assessment from perspective of various stakeholders
10.7   Implement periodic program evaluations
  10.71   Articulate standards for measuring effectiveness of assessment program

Writing Statements of Learning Outcomes

Statements of learning outcomes are fundamental to a transparent assessment process. Stating learning outcomes that are assessable, however, can take practice.

Here are two examples of outcome statements for someone who is to be assessed for her knowledge of psychology at an undergraduate level:

- Can write a ten-page essay explaining differences between Freud and Jung as expressed in one of the following texts: x, y, or z
- Can apply at least two models of psychodynamic analysis to analyze family relationships

A good outcome statement suggests the level of learning that is expected as well as the area of content without being too specific so that one's learning can only fit into predefined boundaries. In addition, a useful outcome statement should suggest but not prescribe possible evidence. In the absence of articulated learning outcomes for any given domain of creditable learning, the risk of an arbitrary or idiosyncratic assessment of someone's knowledge or skills is great. With good outcome statements, both assessors and individuals being assessed are converging on the same point from different directions—the assessor with a judgment on the individual's knowledge or skill leading to a decision regarding credit or credentialing, and the individual with the gathering or creating of evidence of his/her learning shaped by the outcomes by which it will be evaluated.

Without the benefit of articulated outcome statements, assessors may inadvertently ask learners to demonstrate learning at a level that is above or below the standards applied to course-based students as well within a broader or narrower scope. Much flows from well-framed learning outcome statements: additional specific criteria as well as agreements between program, assessors, and students regarding expectations, possibilities, and boundaries for evidence.

The first of the two examples has several problems with it—the nature of the evidence is prescribed (in a ten-page essay), the level of performance is ambiguous (the student must demonstrate understanding), the scope is unclear (the student is asked to explain differences), and the sources of acceptable information is restricted. This statement leads at once to an assessment that is overly broad and simultaneously restrictive such that it would accommodate only a small population of people who may have delved into psychology on their own. The second example asks for a level of learning for which additional criteria may be readily available ("analysis"), a scope that is probably representative of many undergraduate curricula ("at least two models"; "family dynamics"), and an open set of possibilities as to how these outcomes may be demonstrated.

APPENDIX

F

Prior Learning Assessment Preparation (Portfolio) Courses or Workshops: An Outline of Possible Elements

Programs vary widely in how they introduce students to the meaning and possibilities of prior learning assessment (PLA). Across that spectrum are offerings to students of printed materials with workbook-like or step-by-step directions for the identification and documentation of possible creditworthy learning from experiences to credit-bearing courses that are required at any early stage of the degree program.

Below is a sample menu of outcomes for a PLA preparation activity. Some or all of these outcomes can form the curriculum for students preparing the evidence for an assessment of their learning for credit or certification.

The term *portfolio* is used here as a generic reference to the production and compilation of such evidence and documentation, although many programs use terminology other than portfolio to describe their PLA activities.

Ten Outcomes of a PLA Preparation Course:
Participants will be able to . . .

- Articulate educational goals and plans as a context for the assessment of one's experiential learning
- Identify events and experiences that have contributed to one's learning
- Understand the system by which experiential learning is assessed in one's program or organization
- Apply one or more models of how adults learn from experience to the analysis of events and experiences in one's life
- Identify possible and appropriate forms of evidence to document one's claims of creditable learning
- Produce evidence of one's learning that is acceptable to the institution or program and amenable to assessment
- Apply criteria for determining the college-level qualities of one's learning

- Know and use the program-specific forms and formalities for submitting evidence of learning for assessment
- Use the outcomes of a learning assessment process to plan future educational and/or professional activities
- Establish a working relationship with an advisor (staff or faculty member) for ongoing identification and development of evidence for the assessment of one's learning

Distinguishing among Learning Outcomes, Learning Activities, and Evidence of Learning

The dependence of assessment on the measurement of learning outcomes makes the distinctions among outcomes, learning activities, and the evidence or documentation of learning (i.e., learning products) important to keep in mind. These three components of a typical learning situation are easily confused. Below are some simple questions that illustrate the distinctions:

Learning Outcome: *What is it that a person knows and/or can do?*

Learning Activities: *What strategies or processes led to the outcome(s)?* (e.g., attendance at a class, workshop, lecture; original research or independent information gathering; reading; discussion and consultation with experts; experiences . . . reflected on)

Evidence of Learning: *What is a tangible product that illustrates or documents the learning outcome?* (e.g., a product, portfolio, performance)

It is the learning outcome(s) that warrants consideration as creditable learning, not the activity or the production of evidence per se. This is analogous to avoiding providing credit or credentialing for experience rather than the learning from experience. The criteria by which learning outcomes are measured are not the same as the evidence itself. For example, writing a paper is a form of evidence; the criteria for assessing the work might involve the level of analysis, synthesis of ideas, supporting generalizations, and the like.

Regional Accrediting Associations and Commissions in the United States

New England Association of Schools and Colleges (NEASC)
(Connecticut, Maine, Massachusetts, New Hampshire, Rhode Island, Vermont)
> Sanborn House
> 15 High Street
> Winchester, MA 01890   617.729.6792
> www.neasc.org

Southern Association of Colleges and Schools, Commission on Colleges
(Alabama, Florida, Georgia, Kentucky, Louisiana, Mississippi, North Carolina, South Carolina, Tennessee, Texas, Virginia)
> Commission on Colleges
> 1866 Southern Lane
> Decatur, GA 30033-4097   404.329.6500
> www.sacscoc.org

Northwest Association of Schools and of Colleges and Universities
(Alaska, Idaho, Montana, Nevada, Oregon, Utah, Washington)
> Commission on Colleges and Universities
> 8060 165th Avenue, NE
> Suite 100
> Redmond, WA 98052   425.558.4224
> www.nwccu.org

North Central Association of Colleges and Schools
(Arizona, Arkansas, Colorado, Illinois, Indiana, Iowa, Kansas, Michigan, Minnesota, Missouri, Nebraska, New Mexico, North Dakota, Ohio, Oklahoma, South Dakota, West Virginia, Wisconsin, Wyoming)
> The Higher Learning Commission
> 30 North LaSalle Street
> Suite 2400
> Chicago, IL 60602-2504   800.621.7440
> www.ncahigherlearningcommission.org

Middle States Association of Colleges and Schools
(Delaware, District of Columbia, Maryland, New Jersey, New York, Pennsylvania, Puerto Rico, Virgin Islands)

> Commission on Higher Education
> 3624 Market Street
> Philadelphia, PA 19104   215.662.5606
> www.msche.org

Western Association of Schools and Colleges
(California, Hawaii, American Samoa, Guam, and the Commonwealth of the Northern Marianas)

> Accrediting Commission for Senior Colleges and Universities
> C/O Mills College
> Box 9990
> Oakland, CA 94613   415.632.5000

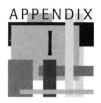

Organizations Promoting Experiential Learning and Its Assessment in the United States

Adult Higher Education Alliance (AHEA)
Director of Membership
PACE Organizational Communication
St. Edward's University
3001 South Congress Avenue
Austin, TX 78704
512.428.1333
www.ahea.org

American Council on Education (ACE)
One Dupont Circle, N.W.
Washington, DC 20036-1193
202.939.9300
www.acenet.edu

Campus Compact (Service Learning)
Brown University
Box 1975
Providence, RI 02912
401.867.3950
www.compact.org

Cooperative Education and Internship Association (CEIA, Inc.)
16 Santa Ana Place
Walnut Creek, CA 94598
925.947.5581
www.ceiainc.org

The Council for Adult and Experiential Learning (CAEL)
55 E. Monroe
Suite 1930
Chicago, IL 60603
312.499.2600
www.cael.org

National Service-Learning Clearinghouse (NSLC)
www.servicelearning.org

Higher Education Section:
www.service.learning.org/hehome/index.php

National Society for Experiential Education (NSEE)
515 King Street
Suite 420
Alexandria, VA 22314
703.706.9552
www.nsee.org

Index